DESIGNATED DANCERS
WHY I DID SYNANON

· A MEMOIR BY ALICE ROST ·

i

DESIGNATED DANCERS
WHY I DID SYNANON

· A MEMOIR BY ALICE ROST ·

Night Star Publisher
San Diego, California

NIGHT STAR PUBLISHER
San Diego, California

Printed in the United States

Revised Edition
ISBN: 978-1-929909-18-6

Book Design and Cover Revision
Jan Carpenter Tucker
www.nightstarpublisher.com

Production Notes
Fonts used: Lithos Pro • Adobe Garamond Pro family
Cover illustration by Raymond Ellstad, Cardiff-by-the-Sea, CA
Originally published by StoryArts, Inc., Leucadia, CA
Original book design by Doris Doi, San Diego, CA

ACKNOWLEDGMENTS

I have often seen the opening sentence of an acknowledgment page state that "this book could not have been written without the following people," and I've wondered if the author really meant those words. Now that I have followed my book from its embryonic state to completion, I fully understand that it would never have happened but for the following people who helped pull it out of me.

The first two people stand side by side as heroes in this process. First, my husband who sustained insufferable first drafts and still treated the book as a legitimate endeavor; who always saw the good, the light and the best of me; and who supported me in every way through the years it took to write. Second, but never second, Emily Hanlon, my writing teacher and dear friend who forced me into the center of myself, through the rabbit hole as she likes to say, and with great spirit, love and friendship helped me do much more than write this book. She is the only authority to whom I bow.

My children asked lots of questions, although they did not get to read any of it, once again legitimizing the project and showing me how much they needed to know. Sarah, Paul, and Kathy, who know who they are, gave me their stories with great generosity and I hope they will allow that I made them mine. Although I did not use most of the interviews I had, I would like to thank everyone who gave me a story. I also would like to acknowledge that there are others in the book who are important to me and may not agree with my analysis of our relationships. I spent many sleepless nights pondering the integrity of going so deeply into the lives of others. In my final analysis that is an inescapable part of the memoir process. I hope I was fair. Lois Sunrich who moves in and out of my life in wonderful ways appeared in an airport one day after about a year of no contact. I told her I was thinking it was time to publish the book and she told me she could do it for me. Lois is also the person who introduced me to writing and the writing community shortly after I left Synanon. Nicole Wisser gave me her poem, which says more about being a child in Synanon in fewer words than I could ever have imagined. And Evelyn Kellmen gave me her essay on evil, which opened my mind to a safer investigation of the subject.

There are as many philosophies about how to help, teach and evaluate writers as there are writers, almost, and I want to thank the writers who patiently critiqued, criticized and supported my work. I also want to thank the ones who trashed and trounced me because I might not have published the book, opening myself to more of the same, had I not survived it during the writing process.

I also must acknowledge that now that it is almost twelve years since I left Synanon much that I felt while writing the book remains unchanged but for some fine-tuning. The one thing that has changed is that I have a new appreciation for the fact that I lived a rather unique adventure and through it learned so very much about myself and people. I do not regret that my path was not linear.

DEDICATION

Why we do what we do
That seems to be all-important.

With that in mind, I dedicate
This book to my children.

TABLE OF CONTENTS

DESIGNATED DANCERS

The year was 1985 and the end of Synanon was in sight. Chuck, the ex-alcoholic founder and leader of the drug rehabilitation and experimental community that had begun in the late nineteen-fifties, was drinking heavily again, suffering a manic episode and making more and more seemingly crazy requirements of the small population of residents. He demanded that everybody wear shirts to work with pockets over each breast and carry with them at all times jumbo mugs of water. Things were getting crazier and crazier—Chuck insisted that someone had moved his glasses from the exact spot he was certain he had left them. Stop everything and find out who the person was, who had done this! He began ranting and raving he had been personally violated and felt exactly as he would have had he been raped. This explosion resulted in his convening the entire population and having them break into groups to discuss the subject of personal invasion and rape for many hours. The few people who did not attend the groups, who went home to sleep for various reasons, were either thrown out of Synanon or "busted" to jobs they had little interest in. It was during this period of time that a party was held at the Home Place, which was where Chuck and his wife lived.

People were dancing in the large rustic Lodge under dimmed lights. Soft rock, popular standards and Latin music played over a sound system. Others were sitting at tables filled with beer and wine and food. It was a small party on a Sunday evening or perhaps it was in the middle of the week. The room quieted as Chuck stood up from the table where he was sitting, announced to the group in his gravely voice that there were only two good dancers in Synanon, everyone else should sit down and allow the two good dancers to dance for all to watch. The designated dancers obediently moved and swayed and glided over the floor to a Latin beat while everyone watched with conflicted feelings. After a bit, the founder's son stood and announced that everyone could once again dance. Some people slowly rose from their seats, others glanced at each other for cues about what they should do, and still others sat frozen in place. The founder countered his son. "Stay in your seats," and told the performers to continue dancing. Everyone watched as this family drama was acted out in a way they had never before been privy to. No one ever challenged Chuck, and his son's words brought all to attention. Finally Chuck bellowed that everyone should leave. "The party's over."

The party was indeed over.

PART I
THE FIRST FIVE YEARS

BEGINNINGS

I lived in a cult for nineteen years. We, the residents, did not call it a cult, and for that matter there are still ex-Synanon people who reject with indignation the word "cult" and all that it implies. We called Synanon "an intentional community," the people business, an alternative lifestyle, a religion. But it was indeed a cult disguised with loud insistent proclamations by the founder that we were doing God's work, saving lives, running a multi-million dollar business while guided by sound mid-western American values.

I left my family home when I was twenty-one years old looking for a cocoon. I have always longed for a cocoon, a place that is soft, quiet and nourishing. Recently my cocoon is my home, a home I have patiently and lovingly created to soothe and comfort my husband and me and provide welcoming nourishment for my children and guests. It is a small cedar house in a luxurious setting of lush trees—pines and palms and eucalyptus. Skylights and doors and windows flood the house with light, and every place my eye sets is full of sky and trees and ocean and pictures and paintings and colors. This outer material package matches an internal landscape I have only recently come to understand. I feel fortunate to have this.

Synanon promised me a cocoon of another sort. It promised me eternal security—I would always have a place in the community, and if I should ever succumb to illness or hardship, the Synanon "net" would catch and care for me no matter what. It was a little like the promise of heaven—things might not be entirely perfect here but just keep plugging, and when you are in need, as indeed you will some day be, then you will realize your reward. The promise was good enough for me. My expectations were low.

Shortly after I left Synanon I decided to write a book about the experience I had because the way I learn is by moving between words and the images they make. I read and I write and I talk. Words are my medium. Others think in pictures, colors, shapes, numbers, even sounds, but I think in words and images formed by words. Even the quiet of meditation ultimately leads me to new words and thoughts that float gently from dark recesses into the light.

So when I left Synanon in 1989 after nineteen years of residency, I hit the books and the computer, writing draft after draft of my new understandings.

During that same period of time my daughter, Elyse, who had spent all of her thirteen years at Synanon, plunged into the larger world with huge appetite, undulating hormones and pathetically few usable skills for life in San Diego. But I learned from her brave, bold appetite for life. I was inspired by observing her daily struggle to find a place for herself in the larger culture, to shed many of the values, mores and behaviors she learned in Synanon and wore like a second skin. She worked so hard at it. I found writing useful as a way to put our lives together. I could work that hard, too. I did.

In order to understand the truth of my Synanon experience, I had to look closer than I really wanted to at my own family and family myths. All families have myths. One of the myths in my family is about my sister and me. I am the bad sister—cold, indifferent and controlling. She is the good sister—giving (to a fault), warm and mushy. Of course, this is pure fantasy and simply not true, but even so, with a subtle change in her tone of voice she can make my insides shrivel and my head swirl with a spate of wonderings about what evil deed I had done, what thoughtless word I offered to make her angry. The power of the myth is strong. Rejecting it intellectually is only half the battle. In up moments I am certain I will ultimately free myself emotionally by shining a bright light upon this myth, and by doing so, let the murkiness and tumult loosen and leave my body to enter the universe that can contain it with far greater ease than I can. In down moments, shattering this dynamic, which like my sister and me, is getting old, seems utterly hopeless. I do know the myth first must be recognized and articulated in order to begin to loosen its power.

The work of undoing the heaviness of these familial emotions is hard. Early in my process I so wished some old and beautiful sage would come into my life, someone in her seventies with white wispy hair piled upon her head, somewhat chubby and wearing long colorful get-ups with chunky jewelry hanging from her ears and neck. She would be an old family friend or distant black sheep type relative who knew my family well, was warm and wise and could help me unlock the mysteries of my overpowering feelings regarding that early life. She would talk to me about my parents, tell stories about those early years that would point out the origin of the myths that powered me with such blinding force. But alas, that is not what my family is about. There is little wisdom, few stories and a complete lack of the surplus necessary to the formation of such a relationship. Perhaps I can become that person for those who lived in Synanon and are willing to break down the myths that ran our lives there. I'd especially like to do that for the children.

A premise of this book is that Synanon was built on myths, not only myths of super human heroes and magical story but also fictions and half-truths that formed its ideology. And we, the residents, desperately wanted to believe in them. Why we wanted to believe in them is an individual matter. That we all wanted to believe is a universal. I hope my readers will at least look at the myths, at how those myths have taken hold of them, and in the best of cases, feel some freedom in having that knowledge.

I have no doubt I am going to offend some people who wholeheartedly cling to the myths of Synanon—a lifeboat that offers them protection from drowning in a sea of lies, their own lies in the form of denial and obfuscation, and the lies Synanon officials perpetrated for years. My intent is not to offend, yet I am not afraid of doing so. My intent is to tell my story, influenced by all that is uniquely me, my family of origin, the culture of the forties and fifties in which my values were formed, my own brand of intelligence and emotion.

THE SYNANON GAME

The game was the cornerstone of Synanon. It was a circle of people whose purpose was to verbally deposit hostilities and anger in its center. This was Synanon's method of examining the negative so we could live positively in community. It was called the game for many reasons: so we would take it less seriously, so we could think of it as sport—sort of like tennis. You played the game for the sake of the game and if there were side effects like stronger muscles so be it, but you played for the sheer enjoyment of playing.

Today, as a member of a larger community, I don't ever miss playing the Synanon game. I don't ever miss sitting in a circle of ten or so people, a verbal free-for-all, bandying about words describing negative aspects of personality and behavior. Never. Ever. I consider this one of the signs of my mental health. Oh, to be sure, from time to time I fantasize being in a room of ten or so people, all facing someone who drives me crazy and wailing on him or her. Someone whose manners drive me nuts, or who lies, is always late, or who just plain dresses badly. I imagine myself stomping on his head verbally, telling her off, whomping him good. Then, after I am finished venting my spleen, I stand up and walk out of the room leaving behind a meek shadow of that person who watches me walk away through eyes filled with remorse. I never fantasize that I am the victim, that the object of my anger will retaliate, or anyone else in the game will stomp on my head. And I dare to say no one who says today one of the things they miss about Synanon is the game, misses being gamed. They might admit under pressure that they would, in exchange for a chance to ream someone's ass, take their medicine if they had to, but they'd rather not, thank you.

The game was invented by Chuck Dederich, the founder of Synanon, in the mid-fifties. He invited a group of ex-drunks who had been through AA to sit with him in a circle and vent hostilities. Chuck, as the story goes, did not think AA was enough for him, enough to keep him permanently sober. He was convinced alcoholics harbored great rage and invented the game as a place for allowing that rage to vent. The game has been compared to attack therapy, and it did indeed consist of verbal attack. Whether or not the game was therapeutic remains open for debate. The game became the mainstay of a small community of ex-alcoholics and drug addicts, the drug addicts soon outnumbering the alcoholics, which grew to become Synanon.

When I first encountered the game in 1966 I was only twenty-four and still very much attached to the image of Jackie Kennedy. My wild hair was permanently straightened and set into as similar a hairdo as I could manage. Small, and well groomed, I even wore a pillbox hat with a veil at my first wedding—the only one where I dressed in the formal attire of a bride. Jackie clearly had made it straight into my body. Sitting in those games in 1966, looking like Jackie, but loving the wild assortment of people I met at Synanon, I thought the game was the greatest thing since the invention of the wheel. I believed with all my heart that Synanon and the game were going to save the world by bringing personal honesty among mankind to a new level. The game was a bastion of freedom of speech—Supreme Court justices would thrill at Chuck's invention. Wow, a place where I could say anything I wanted to anyone sitting in the room and anything I wanted about anyone else.

"Your breath stinks, stay away from me."

"What makes you think I would date a person with the morals of a snake?"

"You have the work ethic of a lizard; I would never hire you!"

"Don't ever talk to me in that tone of voice again or I will walk out."

"You spend entirely too much time with your kid; she's becoming a spoiled brat."

This I could be good at. I grew up with a lot of yelling. My mother was great at it. It was familiar. And hey, I could take my medicine. Getting the game played with you grew character, and you could yell and be yelled at in a protected way with no repercussion. In the house I grew up getting yelled at was much more dangerous and random. The game was fairly predictable. A container for hostility. I liked that much better than the free floating haphazard verbal attacks I had grown used to from my mom. I could do this.

I can't think of anything I wasn't gamed about. My sex life, my relationship with my kids, how I talked to someone during a business transaction that made them feel less than thrilled, my tone of voice, my lack of humor, my lack of vision, my lacks' lacks and more lacks. Week after week, year after year. The game became a bigger and bigger part of my reality, and more and more, long after a game was over, I believed what I was told about myself in games. God, the game made me feel bad. Bad about myself. Unworthy. I could never seem to get it right. And I worked and worked and worked to make myself believe it was good for me, that the reason I felt the way I did was because I wasn't good enough, smart enough, tough enough. I had to work harder. Besides I loved telling people off. I was so angry then. Today when I think about the effect the game had on people in Synanon, it seems so destructive. It was bad enough the adults subjected themselves to this constant criticism, but it makes me sick that we had the kids play the game.

Sometimes the game was a set up. Like the game I was in just before I decided to become a permanent resident, donating all that I owned and promising to work and live according to what would be best for Synanon. It was a twenty-four hour game in a room in the main facility in Oakland, which was a big old hotel and athletic club in a seedy downtown area. The game was hosted by two guruettes. There was only one guru in Synanon and that was Chuck Dederich, the founder, but he was always setting up junior gurus of his choosing to host games and dinners and "get the word out." These junior gurus would be given status symbols so the rest of us could recognize them: special chairs, better housing, personal vehicles, food that no one else got to eat, a servant or two. They would ultimately be demoted, or busted in the lingo, for anything from having sex with someone they shouldn't have, to shooting drugs, to eating sugar when we weren't supposed to eat sugar, to challenging the founder in some way he found disagreeable. The two people hosting my game were middle-aged and that, along with the fact that they had been smart enough to move into Synanon and had status symbols, was enough for me to bow to their superior knowledge. This particular game was intended to paint the vision big and bold for new "square" residents, those who were not drug users, and a few stragglers like me who were on the fence about moving in.

The man, who I thought of as both wise and creative, said to the room, "Alice is the kind of person who when she is looking at the Pacific Ocean wonders what it would be like to be looking at the Atlantic Ocean. I wonder what she would be like if she could just settle on any one of the ten distractions she's working on."

I was sleep deprived and that generic metaphor hit me straight between the eyes. It was true I could never see what I was looking directly at. During both of my marriages, I wondered constantly about what was missing, unable to concentrate for more than moments on what I had been given to work with and putting my head down to develop what was before me. When I was substitute teaching, I thought constantly about my baby Julie, would she be hungry when I got home, how would I get my stinging breasts from engorging and overflowing down the front of my blouse during the afternoon? When I was at home with Julie, I worried constantly about money because her father was in law school and money was much tighter than I had anticipated. In my peripheral vision, images were competing so strongly my attention was in constant motion, everything that was important was in flux, forever moving me toward new and shiny things.

"The thing about Synanon," continued the woman leading the game, "is that it demands total unequivocal commitment. There is only one direction that boat is moving in, and we are all rowers. If you give it your all and row as hard as you can, we will all get where we want to be." She was both rich and intelligent. She had so many choices available to her and yet had courageously moved her family into this community. This game was a softer version of the game. In it the promise and vision and conversions possible to us were magnified. It felt like a warm welcoming blanket. It made me feel up to the challenge of becoming a better person and at the same time changing the world.

Maybe Synanon could make me focus, help me mine just one well. I felt desperate to take immediate action. I felt this might be my last chance to significantly change what I knew was a major defect. I felt I had to act at once. I had to boldly move into Synanon so I could change my life. I continued to struggle for a while after that game. My mind bounced around from the monumental to the trivial. How could I leave the comfort of my own home, the convenience of my new shiny washing machine, throw aside another marriage—Brian was hostile to Synanon and wouldn't even consider moving in. Money was too tight for my comfort; I needed a much greater cushion than my one part-time salary afforded me. My crazy emotions surrounding working and caring for Julie were overwhelming, and the subtext of mothering, looking at my vulnerable and totally dependent daughter was like looking into the face of my own childhood—the time in my life when security and the certainty of love came and went all too quickly. My marriage, not yet dead, was having real breathing problems—our communication was at a standstill as we both slowly moved against walls we could not see in ourselves or each other. I was also at that three-year marker, the time I found a way to move out of all of my relationships. My father became ill when I was three years old and died not long after. My marriages all ended at that three-year marker. It was almost as if

I used these marriages to replicate the love and security I had for my first three years and then left, this time as an adult, to grieve the loss. Swirling in these emotions I had little understanding of, I took my nine-month-old baby daughter, left her father who I had convinced myself would follow us in due time—after he came to his senses—and moved into Synanon not long after that game.

During the years I lived in Synanon I occasionally felt empowered in a game, and at such times I forgot how awful it could make me feel. One evening on a regular game night for the entire facility in Marin County, I was sitting in a game in a room used to store linens. It was a long and narrow building that did not have a specific purpose and was presently used partly as storage and for games, meetings or sometimes special events. The room, not well lighted, was bathed in a coffee brown hue caused by the brown carpet, brown insulated ceiling and beams, and beige colored walls. We sat on folding chairs hastily pulled out of the storage area and into a circle.

Alice: "I want to talk to you, Anna. Last week you came over to the school to hang out with the children, and I didn't like the way you treated me. You hardly acknowledged me when I talked to you and I really didn't appreciate it. If you're going to be rude, don't come over to visit the school and my kid when I am there."

Anna: "I don't like you, Alice. It's as simple as that. I just don't like you and don't feel like I have to be particularly friendly toward you. I wasn't rude to you, I just wasn't friendly and I have no problem with that."

In the game was a man with great personal power. In the early days he'd been a director and on the board, but in later years he'd developed a more private life. He'd withdrawn from the politics of Synanon and did not receive recognition from the executives in terms of vested power. But he was a man the general population of Synanon respected and held with great affection. He used his personal power as a teacher who combined a healthy base of general information with easily-absorbed Synanon philosophies.

Tim: "Anna. You don't like Alice. What does that mean? We live in Synanon and one of the contracts of our residency is that we get beyond such impressions. You simply do not have the right to not like Alice. If we go along with your example of life in Synanon it means I can say that I don't like blacks, or Hispanics, or kids or old people. I can say I don't like a person because she is a woman, or Italian. Don't you see what I'm getting at? We don't do that here. It is essential that we "act as if" we like everybody, at least out of the game, so we can live in community. What you are saying is the antithesis of community. Tell Alice you hate her in the game. Tell her why you hate her. That is your responsibility if you care at all about making Synanon work. But out of the game…she has to walk away thinking you are a friend…comrade…co-worker, someone rowing the boat with equal force. I'm going to give you a 'motion.' For the next month, I want you to go over to the school once a week, when Alice is on shift, to visit the kids, and while you are there ask if there is anything you can do to help her."

Most of the time indictments were supported by other game players. The other side of that coin, however, was it was customary for the game to boomerang back on the indictee so "the other hand could be clapped." Sometimes you got away without that happening. Sometimes you even got through a game without it getting to you, but not nearly often enough.

Sometimes Chuck played the game with me, and those games were usually taped and played for everyone to hear. Even if I did not like what he had to say, any acknowledgment from Chuck was like

14

a gift from God. One such game was in the mid-seventies. It was in a long game which was being broadcast. We were playing the game in what was called the "stew temple" which was a large tin building devoted to ceremonial or long games. We all sat in upholstered chairs and we each had a small table in front of us to place food and drinks upon. It was a room that was given a lot of attention; there was original artwork on the walls and all sorts of Synanon artifacts decorating it. A huge pot of soup, breads, and salads were out on a grazing table for the participants. Chuck was listening to me talk about the fact that I did not think the management of Synanon respected women. I said Synanon paid lip service to equality, but in reality women were second class citizens. Chuck came in to the game to have a pleasant chat with me.

"Alice, which is the more important part of a motorcycle, the front wheel or the rear wheel?" He then waxed long about power and influence and basically set a philosophical framework that glorified the fact women held positions of influence in Synanon; positions in which they could influence the men who actually ran the place. In other words women were the rear wheels, but then the rear wheel is as important as the front, the motorcycle cannot move without it. He was not angry. On this day he was playing the teacher, using my "naiveté" as an excuse to talk about male–female relationships, which was a topic he spoke about and gamed frequently.

I was happy for his gentle approach, but the truth was his playing the game with me in any fashion was proof that he knew I existed. He knew my name. And everyone listening to the game or watching videotape of it knew that he knew who I was. This was a big deal.

Sometimes I played the game with people about things I didn't think were true just because it was the official position and I wanted to be viewed as a good Synanon person, a zealot, centered in the

Synanon ideology of the day. This tendency to play to the audience was especially true in games that were public, broadcast live or shown on tapes shortly afterward. This feeling that I had to play the game for approval may have been the single most potent reason I felt the game served to break down my sense of self. How I played the game became as important a consideration as having the game played with me. I tried to behave in such a way the game wouldn't be too hard to take, and I tried to play the game for approval. In other words I created emotional, intellectual and moral constipation.

We called brutal verbal attacks "cannonballs of truth," and spoken by the powerful and backed by peers they produced a slow, constant breakdown of selfhood. I not only withstood such assaults, I participated in the attack with gusto. I held on to more of myself in smaller more private games, but I got so drugged on trying to get approval, from I guess Chuck and his daughter Cicily and whoever else was part of the power elite, that I eventually had no idea of what I thought about anything.

Generally we were gamed about things we did in the community. Our jobs, our marriages, sometimes friendships. Often we were gamed about the way we handled various situations that were unique to life in Synanon. There were two times the game came too close to me and I drew a boundary. The first was totally unexpected and seemingly small, but it was a significant marker for me and caused me to begin the process of protecting myself.

I was married to a man named John and we lived at the Home Place. I had knitted him a sweater that he wore to a game. My blind great-aunt Dora taught me to knit when I was a very young child, catching my dropped stitches by feeling for them and returning them to the needle for me. I think the process of learning to knit from a blind person contributed to my fascination with possibility,

16

and I guess I cherished the skill in ways I was not aware of.

We were gathering in the game room, which was one of the nicest rooms in Synanon. It was a social game, a couple's game and I had just picked my chair in the circle.

Someone asked John where he had gotten the sweater, which had been my first attempt at knitting after many years.

"Alice made this for me."

I was vaguely aware of their conversation, but heard the other party announce loudly, "She made it for you. I thought you picked it up out of the deglut barrel."

I have no idea whether he was trying to be funny, or if the sweater was actually funny looking, but I felt awful. Just terrible. And it was a different kind of terrible. Perhaps for the first time, I felt attacked more personally than usual, and I decided at that moment to become more protective of myself. I did not say anything in my defense, but I made a quiet promise to reveal even less of what was important to me than I already did.

Another time, much later, when I was married to Jerry, a single woman told him in a game he should break up with me and go with her. Jerry allowed the game to pursue the possibility, and afterward told me he had no intention of breaking up our marriage, but thought it was okay to game it. By this time, I was beginning to know where I stood on certain issues and told him in no uncertain terms it was not okay to game it, and that if he did not make his intentions about our marriage and commitment perfectly clear in games as well as out of them, he was stepping over a boundary that was unacceptable to me. But this was much later when the game was becoming bizarre and Synanon was unraveling and my sense of who I was was coming together.

The early essence of the game that I held onto for years,

even long after the game evolved into something clearly destructive, was you said it, got it out into the middle of the room, and then went about building the vision of Synanon with all the snaggles of getting along left behind in the game. Racism, legal disputes, even war might be resolved when people caught on. On a lesser scale, the game and Synanon gave me the freedom to "wear many hats." Over the course of my nineteen years in Synanon, I wore many images, some wild crowns, and even went naked some of the time.

THE HOOK

It is customary for many of us who used to live in Synanon to recall our earliest days as filled with optimism and vision and idealism, but for me Synanon was a dark place and it was the darkness that drew me into its center. I did not see it as dark, but it was. It is difficult for me to explain to people what made me stay. I was never in love with Synanon. I was never even infatuated by it. The emotional hook for me was inspiration. As I looked at newcomer drug addicts moving from the fringes of the world into health and vibrancy, I saw Synanon as a place where the dull weight of hopelessness that had hovered around me forever could be lifted.

Chuck was the voice of the vision. My introduction to him was at a Saturday Night Party at the Seawall in San Francisco. The Seawall was a big, old musty warehouse that has since been torn down and replaced with fancy condos. The main room, which served as both dining and living room, was the chief gathering place and was set up on Saturdays for the weekly, public open house. Chairs were lined up on the uneven wooden floor where tables usually sat and, in front, a platform, table, chair, microphone, pitcher and glass of water for

Chuck. The story was often told that Chuck personally checked out the microphone to make sure it worked every single Saturday for ten years; attention to detail was primary.

Chuck's speeches were inspiring. He talked about his own alcoholism and how he took his $33.00 unemployment check after a round of AA and used it to start Synanon. He talked about the fact that he gave everything he had to Synanon and had been paid back tenfold. Cast your bread…I have always intuitively believed in spiritual laws and still do.

He talked about what Synanon could become, that because we were people who were willing to change ourselves we could change the world. Synanon was racially integrated. There was no crime. No doors were locked. Synanon had a school created exclusively for children; a place for them to live and sleep and play that was designed so that they would not have to be told no over and over. They would be raised by the community, not just their parents, and be privy to a true extended family. Everyone in Synanon worked. All work was equal. We shared our wealth, our vehicles and other luxuries.

He sat up on that podium, usually in casual slacks and short sleeve cotton shirts. He was stocky, clean cut and spoke with a gravely voice that moved from gruff arrogance to warm humor with ease.

I liked what he had to say. I was young and adventurous and in need of community. I liked that he was certain of the path he was on and certain about what we each had to do to join him on that path. I could work hard at building this particular community. I could work with the kids and, even long before my first daughter, Julie, was a thought, I began to see the school as a way for me to raise a child with the help I knew I needed. I could do this.

Chuck's voice, vision and mandates were brought to us over and over. Every single day. They came directly from him at Saturday Night Parties, tapes we were required to listen to and games that had been taped and edited for us to hear so we got his constantly changing messages. His executives were supposed to talk up his latest plans and schemes in games they hosted and at special dinners. Each time we received some new information either directly or indirectly from the source, Chuck, it was our responsibility to pass it on at the dinner table, at work meetings, with our friends. There was constant conversation about the vision of Synanon and the steps that were being taken to actualize that vision. I was very attached to Chuck's words, and I was one of the people who articulated his vision well.

But even more than Chuck, what most inspired me about Synanon and held me there even when things got nuts were the newcomers. Each time a person who had come to Synanon as an addict celebrated a one year birthday, 365 clean-man days, he or she gave a One Year Birthday Speech at Saturday Night Party. I don't think a speech was ever completed that didn't leave me wiping tears. Young people told of chaos and degradation and disregard for the people who loved them and how by living according to the rules, they were learning it was better to be "rich and healthy than sick and poor." Older men and women told of long battles with prostitution and crime to sustain habits that had taken control of their lives and what reclaiming that control meant to them. It was miraculous—a coming back from the dead. Almost impossible. It was magic. I could do that. I could awaken the part of me I thought was hopelessly damaged.

The inspiration was my hook, but there is inspiration available to us in many places. The other side of that inspiration was also a hook, but I did not recognize it for many years. It was Synanon's dark side that I believe has always existed. Others think Synanon evolved into darkness, but I think it was always there. It was the over critical, punitive, authoritarian, humiliating part that drew me with equal force. There was little that was gentle and nourishing about Synanon—exciting, stimulating, invigorating, yes, with more avenues for distraction than I could ever have found elsewhere, but soft, gentle, nourishing and affirming—no.

The parallels with the home I grew up in are dazzlingly clear to me these many years later. Synanon was in fact an easy, if disguised, replication of my early home. My mother was a complex woman who I enjoy much more as an old woman than I did when I was growing up in her home, which was my home as well. It was a home filled with landmines, which I practiced avoiding with only limited success. Each day, as I turned the key in the lock after school and entered the small apartment, I could feel her mood in the air. An immediate greeting meant her mood was good. Quiet was troubling, and I waited anxiously for a response to my hello as it moved down the hallway into the kitchen where she would be sitting at the kitchen table painting, the smell of turpentine and oil paint and cigarette smoke overtaking the ordinary apartment smells. If she responded quickly and spoke more than a few clipped words, I would relax a bit. Not great, but good. No response, or a simple word or two was bad. It meant that she was in that netherworld of despair, that the house was gray and that I could set off an eruption no matter how careful I tried to be.

The eruptions were awful. A rage that neither of us understood overtook her, and I was too often the target of that rage. I was a good child, so careful to avoid her wrath, I took upon myself responsibility in the house and bought her gift after gift with money

I earned and saved with great determination. She had little to attack me for, and so she went for a part of me that was beyond what it was I did. I was selfish, ungrateful and thought only of myself. I was also told that I was "the problem"…always the problem.

"Me, me, me. That is all you ever think about. Yourself. You. While I work and try to keep this place clean and nice and…And what do I get for my effort? Nothing. Everything is for you. I don't know why I bother!"

Occasionally her rage could not be dissipated with words, and she would strike out at me; a slap across the face or worse yet, grabbing that unmanageable head of hair and yanking it. I cowered, feeling a sense of desolation and hopelessness and shame that lingered well into my adulthood.

But my mother was beautiful and charming as well. During the times she was not angry, she engaged me and I felt great warmth and love for her. I spent long periods in her closet, on the floor when I was very little, drinking in her perfume and scent. The door closed. Out of danger. Her skin was soft and fragrant. She left funny notes all over the house when she had particular foods in the refrigerator that we were to save for special occasions, and in a world of little abundance, good food was plentiful and flowed freely. The good held such promise. The bad was so painful.

I never knew where Chuck was going to come from, when one of his manic rages would overtake him and we would all be held responsible and put through our paces to make amends. Whenever he went on a rampage, I held myself responsible. "Let me first and always examine myself," was a line in the Synanon prayer that insinuated itself into our every action. And since no one could ever measure up to the essence of Synanon and Chuck was Synanon,

I told myself over and over I had to work harder, play the game with more courage, think less of my selfish needs to become a better Synanon person. At other times, Chuck created new and interesting adventures that I found stimulating and exciting. I loved the changes, the experimentation, throwing all cards in the air and watching where they landed. It created drama. It held my attention and focused me on constantly changing new and shiny things, and while I was always struggling with the internal shifts created by these changes, I never had to look at the parts of myself just beneath the surface of those in constant flux.

I don't think Synanon ever truly helped me open up the part of me that wasn't working, that part that felt so hopeless. The two sides, the magic and the darkness, were a balance that kept me at a distance from what I had hoped for. That part of me, more generous and loving, has come to life over the years that I have been living outside of Synanon, and I am certain it is because I have slowly and carefully surrounded myself with gentle nourishment as opposed to the "hard hitting cannonballs of truth" of which Synanon was so proud.

MY DAUGHTER JULIE

Last week I threw away the loosely held together transcript of the hearing of my divorce from Brian, my second husband, when I lost custody of my first child, Julie. Today Julie is in her late twenties, and I lost custody of her in 1971 when she was two years old. I have been carrying that court document around with me for twenty-six years, sixteen of which were filled with constant movement. For those first sixteen years I lived in Synanon I moved at least twice a

23

year. From apartments set up as dorms, to hotel rooms in the big old hotels that served as our clubhouses when we were in big cities, from Santa Monica to San Francisco to Oakland to Marin County to Washington, DC to New York and back—over and over. I packed my precious few belongings into boxes; loaded them on borrowed pickups, buses or trucks and moved. And somehow that transcript made it through every single one. Now that I am settled in the house I will probably live in for the rest of my life, I just pulled it out of a cabinet and tossed it. Just like that.

I have not reread the transcript, but I know what is in it, and I agree with the finding. I agree with the judge who said I abdicated my personal responsibility for my two-year-old baby daughter to the Synanon community. I agree that people of questionable character and morals—people barely removed from jails and addictions and peripheral lives—should not have been caring for her, bathing her and taking her on medical appointments. I agree Brian had far greater insight into Synanon than I did, and that he was acting out of fear for her safety in demanding that either I leave Synanon with her or he would fight for custody. I agree with all of this now, but then that sweet little baby's vulnerability and dependency scared me to death. Looking back, it seems her very existence brought my many sleeping demons to the surface. I felt so inadequate as a mother; all I could see was this magical community stretching its arms out to me and Jules, offering the extended family and support I so desperately needed. Today when I think about that time, I just wish I could hold that little chubby two-year-old in my arms forever.

By the time I had reached the age Julie was when she left me, two years, my parents had established a pattern and dynamic relating to me that would probably have persisted long into my life had my father lived. Mother was somewhat overwhelmed by my normal growth toward independence: my exploring forbidden objects like the loose powder container on the dresser that opened to spill mounds of white on a burgundy carpet, my groping for an easily-opened bottle of ink that I managed to spill onto the right hand wing of a living room chair. Events such as these caught her off guard, and off guard was not an easy place for my mother to be. Her usual comment to people was I was a difficult child and she spent considerable time trying to convince my father that I was "simply impossible."

"To him you could do no wrong," was an oft-repeated phrase from my childhood.

"I was so frustrated with you the day you spilled the powder that, after I cleaned the mess, I decided to put you in your snow suit and get you outside. You were making it difficult as usual (I was two-and-a-half years old), and when I yanked your arm to put it in the sleeve I pulled it out of the socket. Boy, was I shocked to see it just dangling there. It was awful. I called the doctor and he told me to leave it alone, it would pop back on its own with normal use, and sure enough it did. I couldn't tell your father how it actually happened; he would have killed me—after all you could do no wrong as far as he was concerned—so I told him it popped out of the socket while you were jumping around in your crib."

She tells me I was a fussy baby in the evenings after she put me to sleep. I tossed around and cried out, and she ignored me in the hopes of training me to go to sleep by myself. After all, she was exhausted after a day of "…trying to keep up with you." My father, a salesman, came home after I was in my crib, and the sound of his key in the lock was all I needed to calm me into restful sleep. My mother said this happened over and over. Even the hint of his arrival ameliorated the anxiety that already existed from battling my mother all day. I imagine had he lived, their conflict over my management would have produced a somewhat different person than I became in its absence. But I can't help harboring the assumption his softer feelings for me would have made all that conflict and its ramifications worth it.

My father traveled. He would be gone for as long as two weeks at a time. So when he became sick with Hodgkin's disease and went to the hospital for the last time when I was three, I probably wasn't terribly frightened. But he never came home, and the tiny apartment filled with conversation about the hospital and his treatment, who had visited when, babysitters and the new baby sister, the feuding between his family and my mother's family over his care, the funeral and ritual sitting Shiva, my mother's parents, Nana and Pa, moving into our apartment, wherever did they sleep? My life became crowded with the chaos of death and yet, nobody told me.

"You were so young. You wouldn't have understood. I told you when you were about five."

When I was five and about to begin kindergarten, she knelt down and gently told me my father had been sick and although he tried and tried to get better, he just couldn't and was now in heaven.

"Even then, you still really didn't get it."

I got it, but had learned by then never to reveal myself to her. She would have been gentle and caring during that exchange, but at some time, in some rage, my pain would have been thrown back at me in some form that would have hurt far more. I wore a permanently stony exterior before her and never grieved my father. I never talked about him. I simply acted out that loss four times over by being married for approximately three years.

When Julie left Synanon to live with Brian, Chuck gave me a lot of attention. He said I was like Angela Davis. I guess I believed I was like Angela Davis, because by that time, in 1972, when I was about thirty, I had a huge natural and read just about everything she had written. Chuck said that I had mastered "principle over personality." I made a cause out of an event——losing custody of Julie. I liked the attention a lot. I even felt guilty, thinking that perhaps I had let Jules go for the attention. But that is not at all why I let her go. I was just so afraid of ruining her without help, and Synanon was the only help I had. Not only did I bring the tumultuous relationship of my mother and me to us, but Julie's vulnerability and dependency stirred those same feelings in me; feelings I had been working painfully hard to ignore for too many years.

The house I grew up in was in many ways ordinary, but the emotional drama played out daily was anything but ordinary to me. I, more than my sister, disturbed my mother's sense of order, and order was important to her emotional stability. We know now she suffered from depression, anxiety and the beginnings of agoraphobia. It is to her credit that she managed as well as she did. But I somehow triggered a rage that had little to do with me. I tried hard to be good to her. I tried hard to make her calm. I made beds, cleaned the bathroom, did the laundry, ironed my own clothing. I dried the dishes and made my sister alternate nights with me. I bought her presents. But I was never able to quiet the anger, and when it erupted, I was most often the target.

For three years, I had the protection of my father. From all that I have heard about him, he was a kind and gentle man, smitten with my mother who was considered unreasonably demanding and possessive by his family. Of course, his family had their problems as well, and no woman would ever have been good enough for their handsome young man.

My father's death left me to absorb the emotional energy of my mother with no buffer. His family, already estranged from my mother over arguments about his care, continued to see me about once a year, but I was no longer a real part of that family. His mother, my grandmother Anna, never spoke to us again. When I paid my yearly visit to my father's older sister, who lived in the downstairs portion of Anna's two-family home, she would walk me and my sister up the stairs into a darkened kitchen where Anna sat at the table drinking hot tea from a tall clear glass.

"Mom, this is Alice Sue and Barbara Jean."

"Oh, hello," answered the old woman with a smile.

My aunt then turned us around and walked us down the long dark staircase back to her apartment. It was an awkward experience, a yearly reminder of not only loss, but also indescribable rejection.

My father died, and with him the openhearted part of me went to sleep. When I held Jules in my arms I was certain that part of me was dead forever, and it frightened me. Sometimes when she cried, I could not comfort her. I held her and held her, and she howled for twenty minutes or so. It didn't happen often, but when it did I wanted to die or flee. Not figuratively. I remember when she had her tonsils taken out; she was eighteen months old. We lived in Synanon. She was so miserable in the infirmary, whimpering, crying, inconsolable. I fled. I could only stay with her for a half-hour at a time before some overpowering need to leave took hold of me. I left, came back, left and came back later. Her need for me was unfillable. I didn't have what it took to comfort her.

I was assisted in my withdrawal from Jules because I easily

28

subscribed to a Synanon bromide that kids were strong. They were resilient. Changes were good for them. Less, rather than more, contact with parents would grow strong moral character. They're fine, just fine we told ourselves when they cried because we were leaving. Whenever anyone complained about the school, the way their child was being treated, etc. the standard response, after they were told that they were ungrateful, was that the kid was fine. Just fine.

After I left Synanon I was able to really think about Julie when she was little. I recalled my own tonsillectomy, my sitting at the kitchen table, the smell of ether lingering inside my head, listening to my father tell everybody how good I had been, offering me the promised ice cream which I wanted no part of, feeling utterly miserable. I thought about the times Jules was sick, left with babysitters in a cluttered apartment so Brian could go to work, teased in school or simply feeling the pain of a particularly nasty scrape. I though about how she must have felt about my absence from her triumphs. I included Jules in Synanon, but I did not include myself in her life apart from Synanon. I pretended it did not exist, or at least that it could be separated down the middle. Julie with Brian/Julie with Alice in Synanon.

As the space between my years in Synanon and my time in the larger community grew, I became able to feel an approximation of what might have been Jules' feelings. These feelings of empathy, although welcome, were painful. I'd feel them and watch myself shift over to pleasanter thoughts. I felt it necessary to hold on to that ability to identify with my children, but I feared losing it because it hurt so much, so I sought all the information I could from people who believe solidly that mothers should raise their children with little or no outside help. I listened to one particular talk show lady who berated and insulted any caller who even insinuated wanting even a small part of her life away from her young child, callers who were clearly doing a conscientious job of parenting. I listened to her dismiss these people as selfish when compared to me they were headed straight for heaven. This fed my feelings of guilt and made me feel bad. It was how I thought I could hold on to that part of my children.

But after six, seven and eight years of life outside of Synanon, I grew to no longer need anyone to serve as my super ego, as a reminder that I did wrong. I now have my own images that are not going to go away. When Julie visited me in Synanon, she stayed in the school and I visited her like any other Synanon parent. During most of these visits she engaged in the same activities as her peers. I went over to the school, took meals with her in the children's dining room, sometimes brought her to the adults' dining room with a friend, sometimes went for a trip into town or brought her to my room to hang out—watch a movie or talk. My relationship with her when she was in Synanon was not unlike the relationship that other parents had with their children in Synanon. I wanted her to fit into our routines, and I wanted to keep my routines fairly consistent during her visits—partly to avoid calling attention to how much of a "disruption" these visits were. Jules complied, always cheerful, cooperative and affectionate, fearful if she ever made a fuss or asked for more than I could give, she might have gotten less.

She never gave me a hard time, unless I had to change plans and then her spontaneous disappointment exploded inside us both like a bomb. The day before one scheduled visit, Synanon went on "containment" which meant, philosophically, we were going to contain our energies which had become scattered. Translated into day-to-day physical reality, it meant all unnecessary trips were canceled. My trip was most definitely in the unnecessary category. Realizing I was going to call unwanted attention to myself if I tried to leave the property, I called Jules, who was about ten or eleven years old, and gently said, "Listen, would you mind terribly if I didn't come tomorrow. Could we do it next week?" Before the words were out of my mouth she responded with a "Why?" that was filled with despair, disappointment and grief. I told her I would be there the following morning as planned. Fortunately I responded that time to her uncensored need, but I can't imagine the number of times she was disappointed. I did try never to change plans I made with her and, over significant odds, was modestly successful. Jules never acted out the loss of her mother, instead she retreated from it and had little blackouts during her transitions. She experienced lapses in time when her emotions were overwhelming. To cope she simply checked out.

Goodbye was the worst for both of us. It was not tearful. It looked almost perfunctory. By five or six years she had become an expert at handling the separations, and the dull eyes and vacant look had been replaced by bored resignation. I spent the entire afternoon before her departures in a totally agitated state almost incapable of making the arrangements for her return, and it became impossible to drive her myself because fatigue would simply overwhelm me. My husbands helped, as did friends. Everything looked fine, but it was not fine, and afterward I either slept hard or cried huge, venting tears.

Pictures that haunt me are pictures of Jules at seven-, eight-, nine-, ten- and eleven-years-old, dutifully boarding the large van in Marin county on Sunday afternoon to take the one-and-a-half-hour ride returning her to her father in San Francisco. It was on these vans that Julie had her transitions from the world of her mother to the world of her father. This long winding ride, sitting down low between big bodies. Most of the time there were bulky down jackets to buffer her, because the evening air was often heavy with fog and rain in summer as well as winter. She moved alone, from one world to another with no one to hold her hand. No one to protect her. I hope these rides made her very sleepy, and I imagine Julie's little body slumped against someone large, a person who would embrace her and allow her to burrow into his or her arm or side or lap. Perhaps the person at her side put his or her arm around her body holding it securely or even unhooked her seat belt, so she could lie on his or her lap. But just as easily, there had to be times when she sat next to someone she did not know at all, someone so engrossed in his own turmoil that Jules was non-existent or, worse, an annoyance. I can see this person nudge my daughter to wakefulness again and again as she dozed off.

This image of Jules alone as she took the long ride between her two very separate worlds will not go away. So often I hear people don't really change. I have changed. It is no longer possible for me to disconnect so easily from those who are important to me. I no longer need outside sources to fuel my guilt. I no longer listen to the talk show host.

It is clear to me why I was able to so easily throw away the transcript of that hearing on the day I discarded it. I had been married to Jerry for sixteen years, thirteen years past the three years of love I had allotted myself until this marriage. Each of those thirteen years had penetrated deeper and deeper, a little at a time, my scaly exterior that had grown firm during my long childhood. The protection of real love had softened emotions that stood frozen by early memory.

By the time I threw the transcript away, I had spent eight years building a nest for us and for my children. I had a new foundation from which to operate, one created from love and support. I was ready to be Julie's mother now. I could only pay homage to the past by giving her all of my present attention.

One of the stories Julie loves to tell about her weird mother is that when she was in elementary school, a small private school in San Francisco, I arranged to have one of the truck drivers from Synanon pick her up on his way home from working in the San Francisco area. A huge, white diesel truck the size of a small apartment building with the word Synanon in royal blue letters plastered on both sides, pulled up in front of her school. An older black man, his bald head sprouting white fuzz, wearing clean, but faded, overalls stood beside the door of the cab waiting for her. As she emerged with all of her classmates, she desperately tried to figure out a way to avoid being seen climbing into the truck, but the whole scene was on a scale so large she could do nothing but pretend all was normal as everyone watched this kindly-looking, but unlikely man help her up into the cab and drive off.

Jules did not have too much trouble with Synanon when she was there, and she was always comfortable and loving with me. It was during the changeover from normal life to Synanon that things got troublesome for her. For example when we all shaved our heads, she accepted the bald heads in Synanon, but definitely did not want me coming into her school with mine. A generally calm child, she became agitated and talked fast and moved quickly out the door of school on those days I went to pick her up with my almost bald head. When I led her back into her classroom, chatted with her teacher, looked at her desk and bulletin board, she became almost apoplectic.

33

I was insistent, believing my interest in her was what mattered, and never really understood how embarrassed she was by my weirdness. I did not think I was weird, perhaps different or unusual, but not weird, and therefore did not understand how affected she was by the way I looked.

She did not want me at her high school graduation, even though by then my hair was an acceptable length, and actually convinced me that there was not going to be any celebration or party.

"Mom, you don't have to come up. Graduations just aren't a big deal in my school. We don't even get dressed up. I am going to wear shorts under my cap and gown."

I believed her. I hadn't attended either my high school or college graduation, and no one in my family mentioned the missed milestone. I didn't catch on to Jules until too late. She just didn't want me there. I was okay in Synanon, but not in the real world.

In Synanon she had a large group of friends. The girls in her peer group did not fare well and by the time they were fourteen all were gone—either with their parents or sent off to grandmothers, aunts or other relatives. Although Jules missed them, movement out of Synanon was not unusual—it was something the children lived with—and she immediately connected with the next younger group of girls, with whom she remains friends. She also had friends at school. I only met one of these children during all of those childhood years, by chance, at a parent–teacher conference in her school, and it was actually her father who introduced me. She did not want to introduce her friends to me, and I was content to ignore the part of her life that felt so far away. She did not tell me about school events. I did not ask her father to let me know about school events. It would have been almost impossible to arrange my life to include that much of hers. Synanon was simply too demanding.

When she was about eleven or twelve, Synanon bought a large supply of linens and received a huge donation of wallpaper. Julie's dad was a great parent to her, but he has no interest in house beautiful, and her room was a disaster. Without asking permission, which was very bold of me, I loaded a truck with linens, wallpaper, cleaning supplies and several of her friends from Synanon. We drove down to San Francisco and bagged up about twenty garbage bags of old clothing and toys, cleaned, wallpapered and dressed up her bed. She wound up with a blue and white room that was quite charming considering what we had to work with and who was doing the work, and that was the start of a big part of our relationship. I continued to help her organize her rooms and pretty them up, and today she lives in a lovely apartment that she keeps beautifully.

Presently I am an integral part of her real world and we have a lot in common. She is studying to be a designer, and I have loved putting together the homes I've created since I left Synanon. We talk a lot about making things beautiful and comfortable as well as people and relationships.

These are my three favorite things about Jules. I will start with number three because I am somewhat obsessed with the fact that my kids have good hair and have avoided my bad-hair gene. Some poor grandchild is doomed to inherit it, and I tell them both to expect at least one Brillo-headed baby. I hope the unlucky youngster is a boy child. My hair is just plain bad, with no redeeming features in its natural state. It is thicker than anyone's I have ever met or seen, it is kinky and dry, and if I don't do anything to it resembles a Brillo pad more closely than I can tolerate. I go to great lengths to calm it and give it some definition, but it has taken me years to learn how to control it and the battle isn't over because the gray is even more unruly than the brown. Jules has great hair. Elyse, my younger daughter has thick and dark and shiny hair. She can wash it with sink soap and it will dry with sparkles. Jules's hair is just as thick, but when she looks in the mirror each day she can decide whether to have straight hair or curls. She can blow dry it straight or mousse it into wild extravagant squiggles.

The second best thing about Jules is she is not so angry with me that she doesn't want me for a mother. That is because she is basically a decent and loving person with a great personality. Sometimes Elyse and I wear each other out with our intensity, but Jules usually lightens me and makes me laugh. There is nothing better in life than going to a funny movie with Jules. Her laugh is so infectious I laugh from places I didn't even know existed. In the same way her bad moods send me spiraling downward.

The first best thing about Jules is she makes consistent hard and grueling changes. First she is able to get to the heart of a problem she is having, then she is able to figure out real changes she has to make, and then, most amazingly, she actually makes them. It is awesome to watch. She is working on things I didn't even recognize as needing work until I was middle-aged. Where I lunged into commitments and took on responsibilities I had little understanding of, she recognizes the vastness and depths of such commitments and is working toward meeting them as a full adult.

CONSCIENCE

There are parts of me that are very "square," very not-crazy. I am almost always drawn to men who are stable, nice guys. I was never enamored of the crazies as were some of my square women friends when we first came around Synanon—dopefiends who hadn't yet abandoned the swagger and drawl of the street-wise. I like truly decent men, intelligent and well spoken. My first husband was a nice guy. Brian was a bit out of character in that he was somewhat of an angry young man, but a very nice, angry young man with excellent manners. My third husband, Max was, and is still, a nice guy, and the last husband, Jerry, broke the mold when it comes to nice. The only time I was in a relationship with someone who had a more troubled personality was during "changing partners," which was a chaotic time that led to unpredictable relationships. It was a time when everyone in Synanon took new partners because Chuck told us to. But I'll talk about that later.

I had never taken a drug stronger than an aspirin when I moved into Synanon and had no interest in alcohol, but I could pick butts out of the trash with the best of them. Cigarettes were my addiction and I was not the kind of person who could take or leave them. Before I moved into Synanon, I had quit smoking twice—once because I was certain that some day I would have to have my larynx removed and the idea of not being able to speak freely freaked me out—and once when I was pregnant. But in 1971, just after I moved in, when Chuck told everyone that they had to stop smoking, I was doing my part to add smoke to the gray, foggy rooms of Synanon.

Chuck's doctor told him he had to stop smoking because his EKG had come back bad. Chuck told us we had to stop smoking to support him, and Chuck's word was final. In 1971, shortly after I became a resident, there were many more dopefiends than squares (non-addicts) who lived in Synanon, and Chuck maintained the position that but for him those who were addicts would be dead. Part of the mythology of Synanon was that Chuck saved the dopefiends

37

life and for this they owed him. They owed him allegiance and loyalty and trust. He had proven he knew what was best for them and for Synanon, and for this they were to follow his lead. He held immense power. When he announced that there would be no smoking in Synanon, the community convulsed. Newcomers fresh off heroin, who relied heavily on their free unlimited supply of cigarettes to soften withdrawal, bolted in droves. Old-timers, who often said quitting nicotine was much harder than quitting heroin, bolted in droves. The population shrunk and shrunk. How could addicts quit using drugs without the aid of cigarettes? Synanon never recovered. It never thrived as a drug rehabilitation community after we stopped smoking.

I didn't stop. The addict part of my mind, small but active, decided I wouldn't smoke on Synanon property, but it was all right to smoke off Synanon property. That's not entirely true. For the first week or so I joined the rest of the nicotine-starved residents eating chocolate and chewing on red and white plastic straws all day, but then rewarded myself with a few puffs of an evening cigarette. I had thrown all of my packs away, but rummaging through an old purse, I found a miniature airport container with three stale, white cigarettes. After the first week, when I realized that Chuck really meant it, I went to the off-property regime. At the time I was working outside of the community teaching public school in Berkeley, and it made perfect sense to me that I could smoke in Berkeley where they allowed smoking and could not smoke in Synanon where they did not allow smoking. I was not alone in this thinking. I talked to other squares like myself who were doing the same thing, and eventually someone "copped out" and a game was held for all of the offenders who were honest enough to admit to their sins. Betty Dederich, Chuck's wife, verbally slapped our hands and we had to serve tables in the dining room over a weekend, but that was all that happened to us. I never felt bad about this. My conscience was simply not working in this particular area—the area of my little addiction. Once it was clear this was a new rule, and if I continued to smoke, the consequences would be the same as if I used drugs or alcohol, I stopped smoking (in 1971), and haven't smoked since.

For years I said if I ever left Synanon I was certain I would smoke again. I quit against my will, and I was a true addict in my smoking behavior. I dreamed about smoking for ten years after I quit. I had all kinds of smoking dreams. I would wake in the morning confused and uncertain as to whether I had really smoked or not. I was surprised when after I left in 1989, smoking was never anything I thought about doing.

Chuck's doctor had lied to him. There was nothing wrong with his EKG. The doctor simply thought Chuck should stop smoking, so he fabricated the troublesome EKG reading. And if Chuck stopped, we were all going to stop. That is the way things were done in Synanon. Ends justifying means permeated every aspect of Synanon.

Just as my conscience hardly worked at all when it came to smoking, it worked overtime in other areas. Betty D. had diabetes and Chuck decided we would all stop eating sugar in support of her. I have a sweet tooth, but quickly discovered foods with sugar substitutes and kept myself pretty happy with them. I say pretty happy because certain substitutes, sorbitol for example, can cause such severe gas pains that an entire side of your body from your groin up to and over your shoulder including your neck can be in paralyzing pain for hours from eating too much of the stuff, as I found out.

I was driving back from San Francisco after dropping Julie off one Sunday evening. I hated that drive. It was long and windy and so sad. I was all alone and the drive's hypnotic effect brought me inward. The sounds of Synanon were far away. The road was empty of houses; rolling hills, green or yellow, meandered along an unobstructed sky. I felt isolated and unconnected. Jules' eyes went blank again when I kissed her goodbye and because it is far too dangerous to attach words to that silent exchange, I felt it like a dark snake slithering down into my core. I was not yet married to Max, and I had stopped asking people to drive with me because I was so sad that I couldn't talk; and I cried and I didn't think anyone cared enough about me to spend three hours in a car in that kind of silence. Besides, I can just hear the game: "Not only does she spend the better part of the weekend with Jules when she visits the school, but then she drives three hours to get her home, ties up a valuable vehicle and she actually has the gall to take someone with her. Who the hell does she think she is? Why doesn't she just let that kid go and get on with the business of Synanon?" No, I decided to do this alone, thank you.

Anyhow I needed a snack, some comfort food. I stopped to buy a small package of sesame sticks. I'm a sugar person and rarely eat salty foods, but these hit the spot. Crunchy and salty. Good stuff. I wondered why they were so good and at a stop light picked up the empty package to read the ingredients. The second ingredient on the package was sugar.

My heart stopped, my chest clenched with some kind of fear-shame emotion. Jesus. I broke one of the non-rule rules, one of the "small r" rules. What should I do? If I "cop out" anything could happen. The founder's son had been moved from status housing to a tiny module because he had drunk a regular bottle of coke on a trip to Mexico, when it was swelteringly hot and it was the only cold drink he could get with a pretty good guarantee he wouldn't get sick. And that was the founder's son, and he'd had a really good reason for drinking the sugar soda.

But I hadn't intended to eat sugar. Just the opposite, in fact. I decided to say nothing. It was an innocent mistake and I was not going to take the chance of bringing the roof down on my head over a stupid error. But to this day I can still feel that grip of conscience.

It's weird how this works. I converted all of my guilt and remorse over being a bad mother into denial, while I agonized over things like inadvertently eating a product that contained too much sugar. Pretty nutty, as Jules would say.

MAKING A FAMILY

No matter where you live or what group of people you attach yourself to, the need for family, a core group of people to whom you feel attached with as much unconditionality as possible prevails. During my two decades in Synanon I tried my best to establish myself in such a group, and although I did not completely succeed, I did gather a group of people to whom I felt more attached than others. Interestingly, most of those relationships revolved around raising Elyse.

I moved into Synanon in March 1971. My divorce from Brian was final about one year later, and then I was single for a period of four years before I married Max, my third husband. I wasn't exactly single during those four unmarried years. I'm one of those women who is always half of a pair—one man, one woman—in constant search of the "missing piece." Jules asks me why I had to marry all

41

of them, but that is another part of it, the need to be a wife rather than a girlfriend or significant other. I can't say that I completely understand my need for a constant male partner, so I just accept this as part of something I am working out this time around, in the same way I am working out finding helpful spirits instead of harsh critics to surround me. I dated several men during that five years and did my part in contributing to the sexual revolution. But then I married Max in Marin County, California, in 1975 and had Elyse. In much the same way that Synanon seemed the perfect fit, I was certain Max and I were the right combination. We had enough in common, East Coast Jewish families from whom we both fled thousands of miles for independence, compatible interests and energies to keep us grounded, and at the same time a devotion to Synanon. Synanon was considered the third party to marriages, so it was important to feel similarly committed to the community. That way, marital conflicts could be resolved by following what was considered best for Synanon. Synanon was the tiebreaker. In addition, we enjoyed one another and laughed a lot. Just as I couldn't imagine a future out of Synanon, I felt Max and I would stay married because, in addition to loving one another, we had all the rest of what I saw as a formula for success.

Recently Elyse and I had a conversation, and it became clear to me that she had somehow arrived at the understanding that Max and I did not marry for love, but simply because we wanted to have a child. She asked me if I had loved Max, and I saw that after years of hearing how differently we feel about Synanon, she assumed we could never have loved one another.

"Of course, I loved him, why?"

"I remember talking with Max and coming away thinking your marriage wasn't about love, that you got married because you both wanted to have a child and you were dating and it seemed like the way to go."

I wanted to set the record straight, especially if that was the message Max was conveying.

"That's ridiculous. Your father and I had a good time. We laughed and read the same crappy books and worked hard together. To be sure, it wasn't a marriage like I have with Jerry, or he has with Pamela, but I was quite different then. I think if Max says he didn't love me it's because it makes it easier for him to not miss me."

Even after these twenty some years, and in spite of a lot of frustration I often feel toward Max, a glimmer of the lightness and possibility of our marriage hits me and I miss him. Whenever I see him I leave with a sense of loss—not because we so often disagree nowadays and what with all our shared history safe subjects are hard to come by—but because I always hope to recapture a little bit of his warmth that used to belong to me. I am one of those women whose past loves do not disappear and, although the men from my past remain firmly in my thoughts, I suspect I disappeared from theirs years ago.

Max is a doctor. When we met he looked like a hippie, his long six-foot-three-inch frame draped in hopsack shirts and drawstring pants, with long, wild, curly hair and beard, and clogs on his feet. But he wasn't a hippie. He used to tell me that I looked together, but my mind was ragged, and he looked ragged, but his mind was totally organized. He's the kind of guy who looks like he's really taking it easy, while he is doing the work of three people. When we were first married he held clinics in Synanon, was completing a residency in pediatrics and studying for his pediatric boards, which he passed first go around. His residency in a hospital in Oakland paid a little money that he turned over to Synanon and he was given standard issue $50.00 a month WAM, walking around money. We had absolutely nothing materially and lived in a tin bunkhouse divided into six small rooms. The entrance to the bunkhouse opened into a cold, narrow, uncarpeted vestibule where we hung our bulky coats on hooks along the wall. At one end of the vestibule was a small bathroom with a toilet and sink that had only cold running water. It was a shock each morning scurrying down that tiny corridor into the freezing toilet room, splashing cold water over my face and into my mouth as I brushed my teeth. Warm showers were outside in a big bathhouse several yards away.

At that time, about 1976, Synanon had a campaign of "frugality" and we were not allowed to heat any building or room to a temperature higher than 58 degrees. It was freezing, and when we complained we were told the reason we were cold was because we weren't dressing in layers. Once during this period of frugality, I was "scooped" by Cicily, Chuck's daughter, when I walked into the dining room. Scooped means that she asked Max and me to join her at her designated table that had special dishes, silverware, place mats, foods, and came with a servant. I was wearing a wool cap on my practically bald head.

"Alice, take off your hat, we're inside."

"My head is freezing."

"You can't wear a hat in the dining room," she laughed with superiority. "You'll just have to start wearing layers." I wondered how wearing layers was going to ameliorate the cold hitting the top of my bald head, but dutifully took off my hat in deference to her position.

Max and I lived in that tin bunkhouse with a group of doctors and their wives and we had a lot of fun. We were young enough to think walking outside through the rain, fog and cold to communal bath houses in our bathrobes and rubber thongs in order to shower was a great way to live. We were delighted to be out of the cities and small hotel rooms or lower middle-class apartments. Furniture was Salvation Army best and government surplus, and even toward the end, when we bought new furniture, it was sturdy and only modestly attractive. We did not live in luxury. In the majority of housing, walls were made of paperboard, and nails just slid through if you tried to hang a picture. Dressers were frowned upon. Shelves were good enough, and closets with doors didn't exist until the last few years. Everything you owned was out there right before your eyes and the eyes of others who were free to come in and inspect your living quarters. Everything in the open, just like the details of our lives were supposed to be.

The doctors were competitive and there was much bickering and sibling rivalry, but in spite of that annoyance, they talked about a vision of health care, about practicing medicine in a community of both physically and mentally healthy people, and documenting how some of the changes that affected that health came about. They felt practicing medicine in Synanon offered more possibility than practicing medicine in places where you had little control over your patients' daily health maintenance.

It was during my marriage to Max that the only family I had in Synanon came to be. Mary, who is still a larger-than-life best friend, was then a good friend. Mary had moved into Synanon a year or two after I did, after accruing graduate and postgraduate degrees as a scientist. She put that aside for many of the same reasons others did, mainly to be part of a community and movement that seemed to promise great satisfaction and returns on our investments. We talked about having babies together, and she became pregnant without actually planning to.

Babies were born in Synanon, not unlike they were born anywhere else. They were raised differently, but women became pregnant for all of the same reasons they did elsewhere. Some pregnancies were planned, some were accidents, some women were married, some were not. Babies were born randomly, cared for in groups by their mothers in a designated building called the "hatchery" and then placed in the school, which was a separate community within Synanon, at six months.

About two years before Mary and I had our babies, it was decided having babies born randomly was too costly and wasteful. It would be better if they could be born in groups and placed in the school in intact peer groups. Some couples who wanted to have children formed a group that became known as the Breeders Group. About six couples decided to make babies who would all be born at the same time. The experiment was a monumental failure, a subtle reminder to us all that Synanon's power extended just so far. The women became pregnant over the course of the year on a timetable controlled and decided by Mother Nature. The babies were all born within the year, but that had not been the plan.

It was shortly after the last of the Breeders' babies went into the school that Mary became pregnant. Almost immediately, Beatrice became pregnant. She was several years younger than Mary and I, who were in our early thirties. Beatrice's pregnancy was a surprise because she had been certain that she was unable to conceive. Shortly after Mary and Beatrice announced their pregnancies, Betty Dederich, Chuck's wife, told everyone from that point on anyone wanting to have a child had to receive permission from her.

This created quite a stir. I remember games in which women who assumed they would be told no, were indignant and furious. I had little apprehension about getting permission because, after all, I was a schoolteacher and Max was a doctor, and if we were talking about contribution and economic realities, we could certainly afford to have one child. But I was told NO. Betty said I already had one child. And one child was enough. Betty has become symbolic of the soft voice of Synanon and after her death this symbol became carved in rock. I experienced another side of Betty, one I believe existed right along with that softer side, and that is the power-hungry, entitled woman whose greed and need were significant aspects of her personality. Chuck was no picnic. There had to be reasons other than love that she stayed with someone who could be as cruel as he often was to her—often in games made public, so we all could hear him belittle and put her in her place. Chuck held that alcoholics were a higher breed of disorder than dopefiends. He was an alcoholic, she a dopefiend.

I did not have much time to nurse feelings over this rejection, because Chuck vetoed it almost immediately, announcing for all the world to hear that I could have as many children as I wanted because I had given up Julie. Talk about protection and vindication. It was a moment I savored and I can still taste its sweetness these twenty some years later. Saved and protected, such moments made everything else worth it.

The babies were born three months apart, with Elyse being the last baby born in Synanon. Vannie was born first, three months premature with all kinds of complications, and Max and I spent a lot of time with Mary and her husband both at the hospital and after she brought the baby home. Beatrice gave birth to Tamara three months later and entered our lives with a bang. Vannie was a quiet

47

and reserved baby and child, always well behaved and easy to be with, although while in Synanon it was difficult to know what she was thinking. Since she left we have no trouble knowing exactly what she thinks regarding just about any subject imaginable. In Synanon she was fiercely reserved and private. In the larger community she is as fiercely opinionated and stubbornly independent. Tamara was wildly demonstrative and unpredictable both as a baby and child. She gave us the most trouble and the most laughs. Elyse came last. She was very different as a baby and child. The baby Elyse, in the hatchery, wanted only to be fed and fed and fed. She didn't cry much, just grunted about every hour and a half, settling down happy and relaxed after each feeding. I thought I'd never be able to fill her up. As a child she was well behaved and bright, with an intense interest in gathering people to own. Elyse wanted a family of her own and to this day savors every ounce of family she can extract.

These three children, and the mothers who came to include Rosie, Tamara's stepmother after "changing partners," became my core. The kids and the mothers were my safe place, the place for me to do important work and to experience the only truly loving and happy moments outside of my marriage. We were the best team I was ever a part of; we'd hash out problems, come up with solutions and implement them as planned. I trusted Rosie and Mary (Beatrice lived in other facilities), like I have trusted no others in my life. I knew without doubt we all acted in the best interest of the kids, and therefore each other. The children knew we spoke as a united front, not mindlessly united, but united by consideration for their best interests, and that there were no loopholes when it came to the limits we set. I believe this group gave protection to these particular children and buffered them from the harshest side of Synanon. We certainly did not do enough when looked at from a larger perspective, but within Synanon, we were given the opportunity to be model parents.

When our kids were about five or six, Chuck's daughter, Cicily, who was the executive in charge of the school, decided the school no longer needed the energy and attention it had been given when it was larger. The staff was cut back to one full time person. Since it was obvious to us our children were far too young to be supervised by one adult before and after school, we stepped in. Although their lives still looked vastly different from children living in nuclear families, one or more of us met them each morning in the dining room where we had breakfast together before they boarded the school bus. I met them almost every day after they got home from school to have ice cream and snacks, and Mary did homework with them every evening. Mary and Rosie were actively involved with their local school's PTA and raised considerable money for school projects bridging a wide gap between Synanon and the surrounding community who feared and disliked us. A staff person got them up in the morning and put them to bed at night, but one of us helped with general cleaning the dorms, gathering dirty laundry and putting away the clean clothing when it returned from rough wash. The best part of our involvement was everybody knew we were on top of their lives and left them alone to a much greater extent than other children were left alone. I am forever grateful we had that opportunity—the primary people in these little girls' lives after they were six were Mary, Rosie, Beatrice and me along with a variety of stepparents.

The best thing about my marriage to Max is Elyse, who is now a gorgeous young woman who loves words about as much as I do. Elyse and I love to talk. We talk about books and can hang out in bookstores for hours in blissful contentment. Elyse hasn't yet learned to summarize, which means that I get a lot of details, usually more details than I can process. She is about as intense as I am, and when I think I cannot stand another conversation if she doesn't cut to the quick, we have a talk that is so delicious and stimulating and provocative and challenging and insightful I think she must be my sage.

It took a long time for me to understand how injured Elyse is over not having had parents in her corner during the early years of her life. When we first left Synanon I hushed her desire to express bad feelings about her early childhood by assuring her, midstream, she'd had it great and had nothing to complain about. I reminded her that Rosie and Mary and I were always there for them, conveniently blocking out the first six years of her life. I feel bad that I did that to her. It wasn't until she was in college that I told her I had been wrong to stop her, and I agreed that she had indeed been deprived of proper parenting. By that time her specific memories had blurred and hardened into a tight ball of anger.

Once, when she was very little, I hadn't seen her in about three months (the longest I ever went without seeing her by far). I drove with two other people across the entire United States from east to west without stopping. It was a horrendous trip, with the three of us driving for hours at a stretch. We did stop to use the bathroom and ate only once or twice in the car while driving. When I finally got to the school, Elyse, who was just about two years old, had been dressed up for my arrival. Standing in a white pinafore with little white polished shoes and socks with ruffles, she was waiting for me in the adult area between the two large children's workshops and when I saw her, I realized with a sinking feeling she did not recognize me. I knelt down about twenty feet from her and watched her face as it moved from disinterest to questioning to an understanding that

I was probably going to be a good deal. She walked toward me with some hesitation. With approval from a staff member, she allowed me to take her in my arms for a long awaited hug. I knew I had crossed some very tenuous boundary and promised myself that I would never be separated for that long a period again. I was able to keep that promise.

When we moved out of Synanon, Elyse struggled on all fronts. For all of the approval she had gotten about her academic prowess, her work habits and standards were far below what I considered acceptable. Jerry and I decided to move into a school district that was academically demanding (99% of the students went on to college), in hopes of pushing her to a performance level that was more in keeping with her supposed ability. I have never seen anyone work so hard, become so disillusioned ("I used to think I was smart"), and continue to work with such determination. She made friends with other hard working kids, played sports, graduated with full honors from high school and continued to perform with excellence at UCLA where she also graduated with honors. Socially, Elyse was somewhat rough around the edges, and my input in this area was not welcome, so any progress she has made with social skills has little to do with me. It was not pleasant to discover how many social niceties were missing from her repertoire, things she had never been taught, and my instruction was often too late and probably steeped in frustration and rejected as criticism.

But when all is said and done, she is remarkably stable and responsible, far more responsible and careful in every way than I was at her age. I worry she sees idealized family in relationships that are not necessarily healthy, but I know without doubt although Elyse has many lessons to learn, she will always land firmly on her two very sturdy feet.

EVERYDAY SYNANON

Much of the story of life in Synanon can be told through various aspects of the Synanon culture. A social scientist, which I am most certainly not, could take one aspect of that culture—marriage, child-rearing, holidays, work ethic, food and eating rituals—and paint a pretty clear portrait of Synanon. That is not my intent in writing this book: my intent is to make sense of my own experience during the nineteen years I lived in the community and, if in the process I paint a picture of Synanon, so be it. But since marriage and relationships, food, emotional transference with authority, and money figured so heavily in my own Synanon experience, and I am certain in the experience of others as well, I thought I'd give them each a bit of special attention. Although I speak of them as cultural aspects of Synanon, what I am really focusing on are the everyday details of our lives, the little things that add up.

THE STAR CHART

All of a sudden in 1976 or 1977 star charts appeared in every dining room. They were charts—big ones—about six feet tall and thirty feet long and contained in the left-hand column the names of every married couple living on that particular property, anywhere from fifty to two hundred and fifty couples. Along the top, forming a grid, were a couple of months' worth of days.

The dining room was where we ate and gathered for most events. Facing the star chart on a daily basis was unavoidable. Each couple was supposed to place a star, which were handily available, in the box signifying the day and date they had sex.

Perhaps there is some reason other than Chuck's sexual voyeurism for the invention of the star chart. The official word was while Chuck was out and about watching the herd he "picked up" people were not having sex often enough. "Everybody is running around being oh so busy you don't have time for sex." As I said, there might be some other reason, but Chuck had a fairly consistent history of voyeurism mostly in the form of an often loose tongue around the young beauties he always had working for him, and the promotion of nudity in situations like communal jacuzzis and showers, and when we all had to be weighed in our underwear.

I didn't take the star chart very seriously. I mean there really wasn't any way of following up. I stuck stars up just often enough so I wouldn't bring attention to myself, but they did not necessarily correspond to the days I had sex. Max just ignored the entire thing.

SALESPEOPLE AND HUSTLERS: THE BUSINESS OF SYNANON

The business of Synanon was broken into two parts: sales and hustling. The salespeople sold pens, hats, tee shirts and other branded items to companies all over the country that wanted their logos imprinted and used to promote business. This is the same kind of business that Jerry and I own today. Hustlers were people who went out to similar companies and asked for their surplus in the form of donations. The hustlers brought in huge donations of just about anything you can imagine. Food, clothing, automotive parts, tools, building materials, buildings, trucks and cars, TV sets, even cosmetics—tons of top-brand cosmetics.

Both hustlers and salespeople told the businessmen they called on that if they purchased their promotional items from Synanon or gave donated goods to Synanon, they were helping to save lives, because the money or goods collected allowed Synanon to take in more people with troubled lives. Salespeople and hustlers told the business owners their conversion stories as part of their sales pitch. Both businesses were successful. The community was able to hustle most of the goods and services it needed, and the sales business grew to do approximately fifteen to twenty-five million dollars gross sales at its peak. In true Synanon fashion, accuracy when it came to financial realities was non-existent. The management of Synanon could be frugal to a fault in one area and in another spend money with wild abandon. People, at the helm of these businesses, who often had little education, carelessly kept financial records. In sales, real profits are calculated after expenses, but in Synanon we celebrated the booked order and invoiced sales figures. Expense records were shabbily kept and manipulated to give us a tax advantage. Large inventories, from sheets to sales products, were over-purchased and undersold or underused. We were doing God's work, and therefore rules could be bent to that end. Charisma and charm, glitter and glitz always won over hard core planning and follow through.

CLOTHING

After I had Elyse, when I lived in the hatchery with Mary and Beatrice and the three baby girls, we explored the basement of that building to find it was filled from top to bottom with boxes of donated maternity clothing. It was clothing that would never be worn because Chuck had just declared there would be no more children born in Synanon (I will talk about "childlessness" later). But still we were told we could not get rid of the maternity clothes. Nothing was thrown or given away. There was a totally unreasonable policy regarding the movement of goods out of Synanon, while anything coming in was accepted. Once a week Mary, Beatrice the three babies and I would pile into the old Plymouth we were free to use for "outings." We were an unruly bunch and the car always ended up looking like it was straight out of the Beverly Hillbillies. We eventually secreted boxed and bagged maternity clothing into town each time we went and dropped them off at Goodwill until the basement was empty.

Clothing in Synanon was a mess. There was always a general store filled with all kinds of apparel. The store looked exactly like second hand stores look—kind of musty and filled with items that were for the most part just plain ugly or nondescript. Any good stuff was given immediately to Betty, or later Sharon, Chuck's wives, and distributed among the executives, their wives and others of their choosing—the important people of the moment. The rest was left for everyone else. On $50.00 a month, it was not possible to buy clothing, so we made do. I felt a good deal of conflict about the way I looked after I moved into Synanon. My sister and I grew up with family in the clothing industry, and we had always been well dressed, received compliments about how pretty we looked and took pride in dressing well. I liked the idea I could shed my image, but I also tired of the inadequate clothing and the difficulty I had in making things from the store look good. This wasn't a big problem, it was just something that grated away at me every day. I never looked quite right to myself, and nobody else looked particularly attractive to me.

This began to change after I gave birth to Elyse. I had been in Synanon for about six years and was thirty-four. I'm not certain what started the change—perhaps it was the extra pounds I'd put on when pregnant, but I gave away every piece of pre-pregnancy clothing I had stored in boxes and decided to start over—another of the fresh beginnings I like so much. Although Synanon was highly regimented and hierarchal, we had leeway to make such personal decisions and I felt great freedom, power and control getting rid of all those inadequate clothes. I set about carefully buying one of each thing I needed in town, where there were real stores and choices. I bought one item I liked rather than having a variety of clothes I just tolerated. It took me several years, and the final item I bought was a dress—one dress. I wanted clothing that was well made, fit properly and looked reasonably good on me. I couldn't afford gold, so I bought one pair of good sterling silver earrings. I remember this period very well. It changed me, changed the way I thought about the stuff in my life and made me unwilling to settle for less than I thought was a necessary minimal standard. I feel fortunate I have the ability to devise plans or formulas, as I like to call them, and am able to figure out systematic ways of implementing them. This is the good part of liking to start over, of my attraction to new beginnings, being able to cut loose what is inadequate, destructive or simply entropic—even, sometimes people, I'm afraid. Sometimes it is necessary.

But now I'm mostly glad that I was forced to place how I looked on a back burner for so many years. It was a good exercise. I'm also glad I no longer have to do that.

In the earliest days of Synanon, people looked pretty funky— work boots and overalls were work uniforms, and for several years in the early seventies we sewed leisure outfits out of donated fabric. I'm pretty sure to outsiders we looked like a raggle-taggle group, probably a lot like recovering addicts in donated clothing, but it simply wasn't very important. I didn't read magazines. I didn't watch

TV. We saw very few movies. I wasn't bombarded at every turn with inappropriate images of how I was supposed to look. I think that was great. I wish I could eliminate those images from my life now, or at least laugh at them rather than believe on some deep level that I should look as young, as slim, and flat as they say I must.

The kids, too, wore donated clothing, and it was always a mess. For years their clothing was communal; dorms were stocked with pants, tee shirts, overalls and underwear. These were stored on shelves and laid out each evening on the foot of their beds. The children had their own personal shoes, and we tried to make sure each child had a dress outfit, but never quite succeeded in pulling that off. Each time we had to dress them up, which was thankfully not very often, almost every child had outgrown some item, or was missing something essential, and they wound up, again, looking pretty raggle-taggle. Their clothing was laundered in "rough wash" fashion, and every piece sported an assortment of stains. They lived in the country, and it didn't matter very much, but I was always just a bit annoyed at how difficult it was to keep these kids looking minimally well cared for.

By 1975 the entire Synanon School was in Tomales Bay. Before that several different schools existed, one in Santa Monica, one in Oakland and one in Tomales Bay, but in 1974 the separate schools were consolidated and moved to Tomales Bay. Dorms were built. Bathrooms were fitted with small toilets and gang showers, and for the first time, all of the children and staff were located in one place. Since there were still facilities in Oakland, San Francisco, Santa Monica and back east, parents who lived in those facilities and couldn't be moved for job reasons were separated from their children. These separations, some of which went for months at a time, were difficult for many parents. In addition to just plain missing their children, they suffered guilt, and their trust that others could watch over their children as well as they could was often severely tested. They had games to air their conflicts and feelings, but both in and out of those games the philosophy of the school was that we, the parents, did the jobs Synanon needed us to do, and the school staff took care of the kids. Parents were reassured over and over the kids were just fine, that the kids did better when parents were out of their hair, parents were needed to do the jobs they were doing, and they would be visiting in a week, a month, for Christmas. The school was a separate community, with a dining room, classrooms, playrooms and bedrooms. It has been likened to the Kibbutz except that the children did not go home to their parents in the evening. The people who took care of the children were called "demonstrators"— they were there to demonstrate the Synanon way and good morals and character.

It was a holiday weekend in 1975, and Cicily, the founder's daughter, called up to the school in Tomales Bay, and asked that her young daughter be sent down to the Home Place the following morning. I was off on that particular weekend, but I knew that coverage at the school was minimal, so I went over and told the staff that I would pack clothing for the child. I had little recent experience with clothing for the older children and should never have taken this on. At the time I was running the lower school, kids between six months and four years, and one of the demonstrators working on my staff loved taking care of the kids' clothing. I arranged schedules so that she had lots of time to attend to their clothing, and the clothing in that part of the school was in really good condition. Socks were truly white, stains were removed, and baby shoes were even polished.

I took the child, who was about six or seven, over to this big barn—really big—which was filled with clothing. I mean filled. Shelf after shelf was piled with clothing. Nothing was sorted. No pants with pants, no tee shirts with tee shirts, no sweaters with sweaters. No sizes were separated. It was beyond anything I could have imagined. Every item of clothing I pulled brought new information that made my blood boil. Pants legs had been shortened with staples. One skirt had been shortened with dental floss leaving giant holes where it had been pulled through the fabric, another with steely gray duct tape. The kids had taken it upon themselves to fashion clothing that fit in the only ways they could figure out. It seemed so shabby.

But shit, I thought, if the other kids have to be dressed from this mess, so will Cicily's. Maybe if she sees what we're up against, she'll get us some help. It'd take fifty people five hours to even make a dent in this mess, and the school just didn't have those kinds of resources. Yes, I'll pack the kid as best I can, and then Cicily will see. I was both angry and resolved. This will be good. This will get us help. The child was just going down to the Home Place, which was a small picturesque community miles from any city, buried in the foothills of the Sequoia National Forest. It would be okay.

The next day I heard Cicily asking for me over the wire, which was a telephone hook-up that broadcast over the radio. I was in the house I shared with Max and another couple, and only God knows why I had the wire on this holiday weekend. There was little work going on, and most people were enjoying their well-earned time off. There was no way Cicily could know whether or not I was listening, so I ignored the request because I could tell from her voice that she was really pissed. She could have persisted and gotten someone to find me, but fortunately she didn't. When she returned from visiting the Home Place and her father, she put together a public game to which I was invited. It is amazing how fast my resolve evaporated when confronted by her anger. Gone was the challenge this is the clothing that all the kids had to sort through and why should her kid be any different? How innocent and naive I was that I could have been so certain once she knew what the situation was, help would be forthcoming?

"I can't believe you sent my child down to visit her grandfather in that crap you packed for her. Clearly, you are hostile to me and my position and my authority, and the only way you could act it out was by taking it out on my child. I don't care what everybody else is wearing, or how hard it was to find clothing that fit, my kid was going down to spend time with her grandfather, who just happens to be the Founder, and she looked like an orphan. I can't even describe the stuff she sent down. There is no way this could be anything but hostility. God, I can't believe you did this. Can anybody figure out why she would be so hostile?"

I said nothing in that game. I figuratively curled up into a little ball and wanted to take myself to the nearest rock to crawl under. I heard clearly it was I that was substandard and defective just like the clothing I had sent. I was humiliated. I felt both defeated and defective. Every ounce of the fight that had been of such resolve dissolved into self-doubt and self-hatred. It was amazing. I totally absorbed her anger and disdain and dismissal, just like I did my mother's when she raged at me.

SYNANON GOES BALD

The bald head had always been symbolic of shame in Synanon. Newcomers who used drugs or threatened physical violence got their heads shaved if they were guys, and wore stocking caps if they were girls. In the late sixties, the guys shaved their heads to show unity on certain issues, like Synanon's refusal to urine test addicts paroled there. Later on in the mid-seventies, the women protested that for equality sake; we should be allowed to shave our heads when appropriate.

The opportunity came when a construction mistake was made and all of the men shaved their heads as a symbol of taking responsibility for the error. Shortly after, a woman was gamed for an indiscretion, and Chuck piped into the game that we should put our money where our mouths were and shave her head. In that same game someone suggested all the women should shave their heads because some of them, in addition to the men, were responsible for the construction mistake. The result was in every facility women gathered and all of our collective hair hit the floor in a frenzy of buzzing clippers, which resulted in a high of togetherness and common purpose. The result of all this communal taking of responsibility was that all of us, including the children, wore our hair at about one-quarter-inch length for about ten years.

In 1976, at the same time that I shaved my head, I was moved by feminist literature to begin experimenting with some of my own assumptions about a woman's body. I stopped shaving my legs and under my arms. I stopped wearing a bra. I stopped plucking my eyebrows. Some of us began gathering in our bedrooms to learn self-examination where we explored the insides of our bodies, learned what the vagina actually looks like and what constitutes a normal and abnormal cervix. I made a promise to myself that I would not shave my legs until I could look down at them laden with hair without revulsion. It took five years. In this context, shaving my head made sense—and was simply another step toward acceptance of the female self without frills. It was a time to really look at myself without all that cultural baggage. From Jackie Kennedy with a straightened flip, to a wild Angela Davis natural, to bald. I was not a poster child for moderation.

If I had to label this period of time in my life, I would have to call it "The Body," because I also became pregnant while all this was going on. I was quite a sight, thirty-three years old, hairy legs, hairy armpits, hairy eyebrows, bald head and a one-hundred-and-ten pound body that shot out in all directions to a grand weight of one-hundred-and-fifty-two pounds by the time Elyse popped out after two pushes. She was no slouch herself, a little Eskimo baby, weighing in at eight pounds and nine ounces. It is no wonder I wanted to throw all my clothing away and start over.

After we shaved our heads, clothing received more attention. Betty took the women on the sales team out shopping because they were going into businesses bald-headed. This was a really big deal because they were taken to name department stores and not to the discount clothing places where most of us had to buy the few items we actually bought. The women on the sales team got really nice clothing to wear on appointments to offset their bald heads, as if anything could offset the shock of those heads. As we got bonuses and later salaries, more and more of us started buying clothes, and the people with more money began dressing stylishly. We began to look more and more normal, except for our hair. Donations dwindled, especially after we lost our tax exemption in 1978, and most people bought at least some of their clothing. We still had general stores, but they got smaller and smaller. In spite of these changes, it wasn't until the late eighties that clothing for the children began to improve.

Very little money was spent on the children. Their clothing was always donated, and it was never very good and sometimes, like when we ran out of girls' underpants and the officers refused to sign a purchase order, it was very bad. The girls had to wear boys' underwear and they didn't like that one bit. Imagine if it had been reversed and there were only girls' underpants for everyone. I have no doubt the purchase order for boys' underwear would have been signed with no fuss at all. The teenagers and even the little girls deeply resented that they had to have their hair cut short. The youngest girls, especially Elyse, were always mistaken for boys. There were so many small seemingly unimportant glitches we stumbled over daily that seem very important today.

It is amazing how numb you become when you ignore or pass over these small annoyances. I used to think compromise involved the big issues of life. If you didn't steal, cheat, or lie you were okay. I had no idea compromise over larger issues comes only after the ease of compromising the small things. I try to take time now to pay attention to the little things.

TRANSFERENCE

Chuck was the great father figure in Synanon and it was understood that everybody who was anybody had transference with him. Although we prided ourselves on our individuality and claimed to possess higher intellect and consciousness than our "outside" peers, it was widely accepted that Synanon was a paternalistic, authoritarian hierarchy. Chuck often described himself as the father figure. Betty and he were father and mother figures as well as symbols of the integration for which Synanon stood. Their marriage stood for the integration of black (Betty was African-American) and white, dopefiend and alcoholic, soft and hard. The reason we were intellectually able to accept this rigid and paternalistic organization of power was because we fervently believed in the strength of the game, that if we played the game honestly and with gusto, a kind of democracy would prevail.

If you were going to have transference, then of course you'd want it to be with Chuck who was by far the most powerful authority and seemed almost omniscient in his awareness of the people in his small community. He listened to games and liked to tell us that he spent a good deal of time watching the herd. He often told us Synanon was based on transference so if you were going to have one you would not want to have it with some second-rate offshoot. The problem with this intention is that you can't exactly go around choosing the people to whom you transfer compelling childhood emotions. You can't designate the person you want to trigger the same feelings that echo the ones your mother or father elicited throughout your childhood.

My transference wasn't with Chuck, but with Chuck's daughter, Cicily, who was sixteen- years-old when I first came around Synanon. I was twenty-four. Even though I always felt emotions that seemed inappropriately strong regarding her, I never in a million years suspected, nor would have admitted, I had a full-blown transference with her. But I did.

Cicily grew to be Chuck's heir, the child he trusted with the future of Synanon. She was her father's daughter, carried his sword, and spread his word. Buffered with titles and servants, she was given all the symbols of power: the biggest diamond, the largest house,

the most expensive gold chains, the best table, the largest staff—
second only to her father. She stood no more than five-feet-five-
inches tall, but carried herself large, her body language clearly setting
her apart and above. Chucks' son, who he affectionately, but with
contrivance, called his "dumb son," was probably not dumb at all,
but more independent and less willing to blindly follow his father.

When Cicily was in her early-to-mid-twenties she entered one
of the early phases of her training. It was understood by everybody
that she would inherit the throne by virtue of her Dederich genes,
her fearless efforts to bring home Chuck's cannonballs of truth and
her direct connection to the source. But just in case anyone was
confused about this, she was given the title "Princess." She acquired
staff, house, and all the symbols of "office." I guess we all thought this
made some kind of sense. At any rate no one busted a side laughing
at the grandiosity of her title and the seriousness with which it was
treated. But in spite of all of this propping up, I would have been
mortified had anyone even suspected I was so overly affected by this
very ordinary young woman.

Cicily didn't like me. She mentioned a few times I reminded
her of her mother, who had been killed before her eyes by Cicily's
stepfather when Cicily was eleven, an event left appallingly
unexamined by her family and the entire Synanon community. Cicily
often referred to this life-stultifying moment in the same way she
would refer to something as commonplace as her parents' divorce, or
her grandmother's selfishness. This event became a passing reference,
and was sometimes even used to admonish someone... "Give it a
break. God I saw my mother killed. Big deal. Get over it."

Cicily had a big mouth and bad manners. Direct speech was
greatly admired, but in reality direct speech translated to bad
manners and abuse of power. This attention to speaking up, speaking

clearly, "speak up goddammit," which permeated all of Synanon, was simply one of the many ways the game was taken out of the game. Decisions were made from information that came out in games. People were told to do things in a game that were enforced out of the game. Fines were issued because people were gamed for being rude, or speeding. The distinction between in and out of the game blurred to oblivion. It was a mess, and "direct speech" was one manifestation of that breakdown.

When she was fully into her reign, Cicily yelled at me at the breakfast table. It was Sunday morning and I lived at the Home Place with Jerry. Sunday morning breakfasts at the Home Place were my favorite meals. Usually breakfast was put out cafeteria-style and we walked through the line toasting toast, filling bowls with cereal, pulling the lever on the urn for coffee. But on Sundays French roast coffee stood freshly brewed at the coffee set-up and we had home-baked bagels and could order eggs any way we wanted them. I ordered two eggs over medium, and always got two eggs over medium. Not runny, and not over-done. Medium. It was heaven. I still love leisurely Sunday mornings.

Cicily and her husband joined me at a large round table I had just started. The conversation led to a discussion of a video we had both seen. I had liked it. It was a movie called Haywire and it was about Leland Hayward and Maureen O'Sullivan and their family, which was full of tragedy. I said I had enjoyed the movie, which gave Cicily her opening for my lecture.

"Oh, it was a great movie all right, glorifying the nuclear family and its destructiveness. It was a movie about everything Synanon is trying to destroy, and it is people like you, Alice, who, through promoting such garbage, are going to be the undoing of the school, which is Synanon's way of doing away with the nuclear family."

66

Jesus Christ. All I said was that I liked the movie. I also loved Gitta Sereny's book about Albert Speer, which treats him honestly, but with sympathy. Does that mean I am a Nazi supporter? I felt like I'd been punched in the stomach. There I was, wrong again. Cicily could say anything she wanted in any setting in the name of direct speech or furthering the vision of Synanon. The means always justified these most noble ends. I would eventually get very tired of these kinds of encounters and loosening the grip of her influence and anger was one of the things that ultimately freed me from Synanon.

THE COIN OF THE REALM

Many people think the introduction of money, paying people randomly assigned wages, was the undoing of Synanon. When I moved into Synanon most people had no money. Some people, not many, worked at jobs outside of Synanon and handed over their paychecks. The rest of us worked doing jobs for Synanon, and we were not paid in cash, but received housing, furniture, medical care, child care, meals and $50.00 WAM (walking around money) a month. Everyone contributed their all, and only executives got paid. At first this pay was in the form of goodies—better housing, personal vehicles, personal services, expense accounts and, later, they were paid relatively large salaries.

Bonuses were handed out from time to time and that created a mess of sibling rivalry. In the seventies better housing and bonuses had been raffled so feelings were not hurt. But later bonuses were handed out on the basis of "merit" and have-nots were crushed. Why should he get... when I... Feelings were badly hurt in the community where giving your all was supposed to count for something. Later still salaries were handed out and the fun really began. I don't think

I ever felt more rage than I did when some person who I thought was equal to me in every way was given lots more money than I. It was arbitrary and random like everything else, but it didn't feel that way. People longed for recognition for their great efforts and great love, and when they were denied that recognition, or given less than others, it hurt. The only thing that was constant was that Chuck's right-hand people were given more and more money and goodies than the rest of us.

In the late seventies Synanon was into making a fast buck. Chuck had a personal stockbroker, who was my "love match" after "changing partners"—John—and Chuck was certain Synanon could make a killing in the market. They bought a sizable number of diamonds, which turned out to be a not-so-terrific investment, and when we were cash poor and not paying WAM, salaries or bonuses, the executives decided to have a diamond give-away.

Everybody who was anybody got a diamond. All of my peers got diamonds and even people in Synanon less time than I did. I did not get a diamond. I'm certain it was either an honest oversight, or an opportunity for someone—like the founder's wife, Sharon, with whom I'd had an antagonistic relationship before her marriage to Chuck—to take a chunk of revenge. After a very short spell of feeling left out, while everyone was picking settings for rings, I decided to buy my own diamond, which I did several days later. I had always been a saver, and over the years had put away much of the money I'd been given. Most of the diamonds given out at the give-away were small and I bought a diamond that was much bigger than one I would have been given. I made certain that I sparkled with everyone else.

You were supposed to get what you needed from Synanon, but the catch was some official was always in the position of deciding what it was you needed. Jerry, long before he became my last husband, had saved Synanon tens of thousands of dollars by examining phone bills and isolating billing errors. Jerry had an MBA from UCLA and has an astute business head. His major contribution to Synanon was his indefatigable effort to balance sound business practices with the "Synanon way." Jerry's father died after a long illness, and he asked for airfare to the East Coast to attend the funeral. I guess this didn't count as need, because he was given the fare in the form of a loan.

The executive committee member to whom Jerry reported responded to his request. "We can advance you the $350.00 and attach it to your motorcycle loan."

"That's not what I had in mind. I think I should be given the money because it is a family emergency and because I have earned that money over and over by the work I do."

"Take the loan. I could say no."

Jerry knew then, with that ever-correct first voice, he was living in the wrong place, but immediately translated the thought into a common mantra. "I don't live in the same Synanon as Tom, Chris, John (whoever was making the decision). I live in Chuck's Synanon. If Chuck only knew. But you can't just bring every little issue to Chuck. He is too busy with matters of much greater importance than my little $350.00. I'll pay it back. No big deal."

I understand "If Hitler only knew" was also a common phrase used by his officials when they, too, thought things were not as they should be.

FOOD

Food in Synanon was a really big deal, as it is for most people, but we spent hours in Synanon sitting around tables talking and eating. Most social gatherings revolved around eating, and events put on by Chuck or his executives were often eating feasts. As the years progressed rituals surrounding food became more and more significant.

I could never have known that choosing the amount of food I ate at any given time was important to me until "portion control." Shortly after I moved into Synanon, in 1970, cooking in dorms or apartments was stopped, and the only place you could eat was in the big central dining rooms, which in my case was in an old hotel ballroom in a rundown section of downtown Oakland. The room was huge with painted ceilings that were several stories above the floor. We sat at large round tables with anyone we wanted, except for two VIP tables set at one end that were reserved for the directors and their invited guests. The kitchen was out of sight, but on one end of the large room, there was a long food line with servers on one side and diners lined up on the other. Waste became an issue as the community moved from individual kitchens to a more institutional approach, so portion control came to be. It worked this way: I walked through the food line, looked into the face of some burly Italian from New York, thick black hair straining over the collar of his starched white jacket, who stood poised, serving spoon in hand.

"I just want a very small amount of that stew, like a couple of tablespoons, please."

In response to this, he piled enough stew on my plate to feed a small village. Then, when I went to bus my dishes, which still overflowed with stew, I was "pulled up" for wasting food.

This kind of double-bind in which all choices seemed to contradict one another, was repeated over and over. Dopefiends were hostile to the squares who were invading their happy home. Crazy people were given little bits of power, "I can give you as much food as I want and you can't do anything about it." And residents were in constant quandaries trying to negotiate virtual land mines. It was pretty crazy, but the craziness, as always, was tempered by the feeling that we were breaking ground. After all, we were inventing a new way to organize the structure of our community so that I would never have to cook a meal again if I didn't want to. Never have to think about menu planning, preparation time and, worst of all, clean up. I was ready to make small sacrifices for that freedom. Even today, I have the world's most perfect take-out kitchen. Jerry considers it a special evening when I actually put together a meal from scratch.

We had airline meals donated, thousands of airline meals, and the food service people disguised them in as many ways as was possible, but the fact is we ate airline food for years. Then there was the chicken on a stick, Chicken Dixie, which was an almost-food; some kind of ground-up something covered with what passed for crumbs. Chicken Dixie was on the food line at least once a day for I don't know how many years. I am proud to say that I never tasted Chicken Dixie, that I know of. I was raised on fresh, wholesome food, which we had in abundance. Cake and bread were a constant on the sideboard. Pepperidge Farm, Oreos, Malomars, and chocolate-covered graham cracker cookies were stored in bags over the broom closet, and the refrigerator always contained fresh fruit. My mother prepared meals from scratch each evening. She wasn't the world's greatest or happiest cook, but we never wanted for good food. Early on in Synanon, I began eating salads laced with tuna or hard-boiled eggs when I could get them.

The first thing I think about every morning, the image that gets me out of bed, is a steamy cup of fresh-brewed coffee and a piece of buttered toast. Since I quit smoking and could no longer get out of bed for the promise of that first nicotine rush, caffeine has served as a perfectly acceptable substitute. I am not a lot of fun to be around if something goes wrong with that morning ritual. At one point when I lived in Synanon, I started having terrible headaches. I complained at a dinner table, and several people at the table volunteered that they too were having headaches. This went on for about a week. I didn't think much about it until someone complained that food service had received a donation of decaffeinated coffee and stopped serving regular coffee without telling anybody. Once the change was "out," regular morning coffee was again offered.

Another interference with the morning routine was not as easily accepted. This was when some food service genius decided to save a few cents by re-using coffee grinds. Sometimes the coffee tasted okay, and sometimes it was watery and flat. Complaints about the quality of the coffee at that time were loud and clear and once again regular service was resumed.

There were constant, little manipulations to keep us ever reminded that our control was minimal. But I thought this was control over such little things. How important is morning coffee, when you are changing the world? What difference does a little caffeine make when you are saving lives?

We weren't allowed to eat sugar from 1975 until the mid-eighties. The little kids were not happy about this, and the teenagers were practically suicidal. Every once in a while we would be given a sugar day. It was usually Cicily who decided when we would have sugar days, but mind you, the executive committee and Chuck and his wife could both eat and serve foods with sugar whenever they wished. I would say that for every sugar day we, the residents, had the executive committee had eaten sugar on, at the very least, ten occasions. Several times I heard Cicily complain after receiving a request for a sugar day, "All those people ever think about is when they can eat sugar. Give me a break." I wondered to myself how she could be so disdaining when she got to eat the stuff any time she wished. People on the executive committee had this way of rationalizing the vast differences between their positions and the rest of us. I guess they did the same thing with sugar that they did with money. They told us they did not consider the large sums of money given to them as "theirs." The money was in their hands for safekeeping to be used in case anything happened to Synanon. The money in their possessions would be a way of keeping us all together if our funds were ever attached. They ate sugar when they were entertaining. The sugar wasn't really for their personal pleasure; it was something allowed to them so they could serve it to guests. That is what they told us, but the everyday reality was that they were materially way better off than the rest of us and could eat sugar... however they rationalized it.

On sugar days, from morning until night, every dining room dripped with sweets. Pancakes with maple syrup all day long. Ice cream, candy, jelly, cake, donuts. All day long, as much as you wanted. People sat with soup bowls filled with ice cream, several times over. I hated sugar days. I hated the swing between deprivation and indulgence. All I wanted was to be able to have some small sweet a couple of times a day. I thought sugar days were sick. All or nothing—moderation was a dirty word.

Then there were the fad diets. I often wonder what the doctors who participated now think about these diets. There was the oil diet on which you could eat as much fat, any kind of fat, and protein as you wanted. That's all—just fat and protein. People ate chicken, steaks, tuna fish soaked in olive oil or mayonnaise. I saw some people drink olive oil out of a water glass.

When diets failed to bring desired weight loss, as they always did, we had the fat-a-thons. Chuck, his second wife, Cicily and many others ranged from chubby to obese. The fat-a-thons were designed to help them and others lose weight. Ideal weights were pulled from some obscure insurance company chart, and weigh-ins were called to make sure we were all moving towards these weights, which were extremely low by any standards.

Weigh-ins, which were held periodically throughout weight loss periods, were early morning ceremonies. Large gathering rooms were set up with scales. Doctors and nurses, assistants and people appeared in their underwear: bras and panties for the women and underpants for the men. Everyone was weighed in an orderly fashion. A luxurious breakfast was available, music played and people milled, waiting to be weighed in their very best underwear. I bought a new set for the first weigh-in and designated that particular set of underwear for weigh-ins only. At some of the weigh-ins each person was looked over by the doctors and told how much more weight they had to lose. There were people who did a last-minute push before they were to be weighed. One woman I know fasted the day before she was to be weighed, ran miles, spitting along the way to eliminate as much water as possible, and ended her day in a sauna wearing plastic rain gear and rain boots with the intention of sweating out the last ounce of water weight.

At one weigh-in, in a spontaneous burst of enthusiasm, someone took off her bra and within minutes the entire Tomales Bay population—all three properties—was nude. This was the one and only nude weigh-in. This sudden nudity upset some people, and games were set up for them to discuss their feelings. The games were held in the nude. The kids were not permitted to attend weigh-ins, but Elyse tells me they took turns peeking in windows. Some of the teenagers were told they had to lose weight and because of this consumed fewer calories and less nutrition than their growing bodies needed.

If you didn't lose weight in a given period of time, you could be punished, like the young woman who was sent home from a sales trip and "busted" because she was weighed and hadn't lost anything. The food line changed when we were having these weight loss periods, and mashed cauliflower, diet jello and salad were served in abundance. I felt like I was starving. The first fat-a-thon started shortly after I gave birth to Elyse, so I welcomed the chance to get help losing all the weight from the pregnancy, but once I lost it, I just longed for real food.

Recently I looked over twenty years of Synanon photos someone had collected and catalogued. You could see the changes that took place over the years, the early building years with young people on heavy equipment digging trenches and laying pipe, years of pictures of infants and children when the school was in its heyday; and then there were the pictures from the fat-a-thon years where people I know and love look like shadows of themselves. Terribly underweight and shorn. I found looking at the pictures of all those ultra thin, bald people disturbing.

Again, after weigh-ins there were either sugar days or huge meals served in celebration of having lost weight. Sort of like my rewarding myself with a cigarette after not smoking all day. One Christmas we all weighed in during the morning, in our underwear, and then later that day sat down for an incredible feast. One young man at my dinner table gained eleven pounds in that one day.

Broth and bran was a before-meal ceremony that went on for several years starting in 1976. It was decided that we needed more bran in our diets. This was followed by the invention of various ways to get the dreadful sawdust-like stuff down our throats. It was baked into our homemade breads, which were delicious, and the broth and bran ceremony was invented. Before each meal we ate a small bowl of broth mixed with several tablespoons of bran. People on sales trips all over the country had to take along enormous bags of bran to fulfill their dietary obligation while on the road. I once walked into a hotel suite that was being used as a family room for a dozen or so salespeople on a trip, and the bathtub was filled with fifty-pound sacks of bran. Everyone on the trip took little plastic bags of bran into restaurants to mix into soup or pour over salads.

Needless to say there was abundant conversation about the digestive process during this period, especially at our daily gatherings around dining room tables. One of the sub-topics was "transit time"—the time it takes for food to be digested and its waste eliminated. Transit time was an important factor in determining digestive health. How to assess whether or not you had a good rather than bad transit time? We were all to eat tiny yellow millet seeds, watch for them in our stools, and when we spotted the undigested yellow dots, we would know our transit times. Table talk was fascinating.

Anyone who has tried to change their diet knows how elementally important food is, and how deeply involved we are with eating patterns established early in life. These are only a few of the more flamboyant food maneuvers, and at the time I was so grateful I did not have to prepare daily meals, I was willing to accept any and all food machinations. Today, as I eat what I like, when I like, I rejoice in the freedom to choose, and the fact that I have to put up with grocery shopping, food preparation and clean up seems a small price to pay.

PART II
CHANGING PARTNERS

CHANGING PARTNERS

CHANGING PARTNERS

Today, I frequently feel like an impostor as I present myself packaged in conventional form, hair well-cut, body trim, good clothing, nice house, successful business and well-married; a middle-aged woman of means. I meet someone new and we get to talking about our lives and when I am certain this new person generalizes what she sees in me backward to a young wife and mother raising family, building the life she now sees, I remember "changing partners" and the walls come crumbling down. What do I tell her? How many times have I been married? How does honesty and privacy overlap and where do I draw the line? Do I have to tell about "changing partners," and how the hell does one tell a stranger to the ways of cults about "changing partners," when it has taken me over twenty years to understand it myself?

As I move into the story of changing partners, it is important to understand that when we moved in to Synanon we were asked to abandon all commitments. We gave everything we owned, including all of our money, to Synanon and were told "it doesn't take much of a man, it just takes all of him." Family, including children living outside, were to be set aside so that full attention could be given to the work of Synanon, changing ourselves and thus changing the world. Even within the community, contracts held between friends, spouses and co-workers were to be broken in games. Principle over personality was a popular slogan. Our total commitment, which was based upon blind trust—"Trust is a way of knowing"—was demanded in every way.

Give up all of your commitments and commit to Synanon doesn't make much sense if you think about it for more than a minute. True commitments aren't that easily cast aside, but since we had all done it once when we moved in, and then again and again after residing in Synanon, it wasn't that big a leap to changing partners.

MAX

Although Max and I were a stable and happy couple in Synanon, we had developed the bad habit of practicing small meannesses with each other. One of the contracts we held that did nothing for the growth of our relationship was that Max was less committed to Synanon than I, and that I was less competent than Max. Max questioned Synanon assumptions and policies more than I did and maintained more independence than I. Toward the end, after I was married to Jerry, Max worked outside of Synanon as a doctor, and decided what portion of his income he was going to keep and what he was going to donate to Synanon, which created quite a stir. He bought disability insurance and set up a trust fund for Elyse's college education, which, in addition to serving Elyse, has been a gift to me as well. He exercised his independence more than most of us, and perhaps that is why he has so many more good feelings about Synanon than I do.

I am less competent than he is in the work world—in getting the job done. For years I felt bad about this until I recently discovered I am a writer and was shriveling up trying to be some kind of organized superwoman. We gamed each other about these assumptions all the time and I had the upper hand because I had given up custody of Jules, which was proof of my commitment, and it was easy to accuse Max of whining because he questioned things in a community that demanded complete conformity.

Something of profound significance happened in Synanon

during our marriage, and in retrospect, the way we handled an issue of such great personal magnitude revealed a lot about the kind of relationship we had. When I was about seven months pregnant with Elyse, Chuck decided we would stop having children in Synanon. There would be no more children born into the community, and instead of having our own we would take care of the world's unwanted children. Every edict was always wrapped tightly in some visionary philosophy only a Philistine could argue with. Four women were carrying babies, anywhere from a few weeks to four months, and they all had abortions. They were told to have abortions. I've heard one of the women was taken aside by Chuck's wife, Betty, and told that she did not have to, but they all did.

I didn't think much at all about those women at the time. How could I, waddling around about to burst with baby? But now it seems so cruel. Three of the women were in their thirties and never did have children. One was a bit younger and now has a family. One of them was four months pregnant and delivered a non-viable child with thick black hair after labor was induced. In addition to the abortions, to facilitate "childlessness," all men over the age of eighteen who had been in Synanon for more than five years were to have vasectomies.

Max's initial response—in a game—was, "I'm not certain that I want to do this. It's a pretty absolute decision...the possibility of reversing vasectomies is not always that great and I'm not so sure I want to give up the ability to have more children."

"But do you want to have another child," I asked, knowing full well I was not going to have a third child.

"I don't think so. But a vasectomy is so absolute."

"Oh, Max, this is just another example of your equivocating over every commitment. You don't really want to have another child. You're just dragging your heels as usual. This is ridiculous. You don't even want another child and you're wasting everybody's time complaining about doing something which will simply ensure that you don't. Why can't you look at the bigger picture?"

I don't recall any conversations we had out of the game about his having a vasectomy. I never asked about his fears and doubts. Did he have fantasies about having a son? Did he worry his parents would be denied the possibility of another grandchild? Did he wonder what he would do if anything happened to Elyse? I was completely uninterested in his conflict, and it is just as well, for had I heard him out with empathy, it might have led to leaving, and for reasons that to this day remain unclear, I just couldn't do that. Max had his vasectomy and, along with the other doctors, was trained to do the procedure. He performed many vasectomies on the boys and men of Synanon and I assisted.

It's funny how things turn out. I feel no loyalty to any part of Synanon or any person attached to Synanon simply because they were part of that community. I have no interest in keeping family skeletons in their closets. I am committed to balance, to looking at both the dark and the light, to finding the truth as it exists apart from falsehood and illusion. I am finding my stride as an artist. Max is deeply committed to many aspects of Synanon and his experience there, and he remains competent in his work.

CHANGING PARTNERS: OVERVIEW

Max and I were married just short of three years when we changed partners. Elyse was about eighteen-months old and Jules was seven. By this time the original two rules of Synanon, which were no drugs or alcohol and no physical violence or threats of physical violence, had mushroomed into many mandates. Even though we had to do mandatory aerobic exercise and wear overalls to work, play at least one Synanon game a week, were forbidden to smoke, eat sugar, wear our hair more than one-quarter-inch long or procreate, we still maintained there were only two rules in Synanon and we were governed by some kind of group process.

In 1977 Betty Dederich died of lung cancer and several months later Chuck married a much younger woman named Sharon. Since Chuck couldn't do anything by himself, he began talking to the people in his inner circle, including his son and daughter, about ending their tired marriages and starting over with him.

Your marriages are relationships of habit. I've played games with you for years and years and heard the same tired complaints. He's too tired for sex. She always puts her foot in her mouth and is inappropriate. Things that never change. Scratches on the blackboard that are so deep they cannot be written over. There are too many scratches on the blackboard. We need some new blackboards to write new scripts on. We all need to learn how to cherish another person, like a child cherishes a doll. The child learns to love the doll by cherishing it. You can learn to love anyone in Synanon simply by cherishing them.

He was learning so much about how to start a relationship fresh he was compelled to include others in his experience. One thing led to another, the dissolution of one marriage led to the dissolution of another, and within weeks it became apparent we were all going to change partners, so we'd better figure out a way to wrap our minds around it. As usual Chuck, in his greater wisdom, was asking of us not to understand but to trust him, or at least to do what he said or leave. That was basically the only option.

Even though, by my present standards, personal commitments in Synanon were flimsy at best, those of us whose marriages were threatened by this new tidal wave experienced turbulent emotions. One moment people were joking they were going to go to the mattresses on this one, and the next crying on one another's shoulders. I insisted Chuck couldn't mean everybody, I mean people like Max and me who'd been together a relatively short time, and wanted to stay married, we'd surely be able to. At other moments I tapped into my inherent infatuation with new beginnings. Clean slates. Second chances to do things right.

The atmosphere of Synanon was infused with a communal vulnerability, and with everyone unsettled and agitated and confused, the climate of Synanon changed. Our vulnerability drew us together in a way I had not experienced before, and the mutual distrust that grew out of knowing anything you said or did was subject to attack in a game all but disappeared. There was an equality and sense of connection that until this time had been given only lip service. This feeling and energy was vibrant and not only eased my uncertainty but reinforced the feeling I would do just about anything to feel this much a part of something—this connected to so many people—all kinds of people. Couples were separating in large numbers, and executive committee members, used to privacy and perks, were sharing living space with their employees. The rigid class structure of Synanon dissolved. Women who maintained distance through their authority, title and position plopped down next to me at the dinner table and confided their fears and doubts knowing I understood exactly how they felt. Newcomers who had been in Synanon a few short months took over the running of the facility—distributing the mail, running the food service operation, maintaining the facility. They thought everyone had gone nuts and many rose to the occasion.

The initial wave of changing partners couples were mostly people who had been married for what in Synanon we considered a long time, five, eight or ten years. When it became evident that newer marriages were going to have to break up, Chuck coined the phrase, moving from peak to peak. Why wait until a marriage deteriorates? If you leave from a high point, you can begin the new relationship at a high point.

I understand why I changed partners, but I grieve for that young woman who so misunderstood connection she was able to give up what might have been substantially real for some passing high. I often think of the conversations I should have had with Max that would have helped him develop his thoughts on specific issues instead of throwing everything back at him as mere reflections of his lack of commitment. I think those conversations, that sharing of one's inner thoughts, fears, conflicts, and dreams is what intimacy is all about.

CHANGING PARTNERS: SOME DETAILS

All over Synanon "Separation Ceremonies," which were ceremonies that ended marriages, were taking place. Max and I along with two other couples had our ceremony in the living room of the place Max and I shared with another couple. Three couples sat on six upholstered chairs that formed a gentle arch. We were dressed in robes. Ironically, Jerry, who was to become my final husband, and who I rejected during changing partners, officiated. There were a lot of people in the room as witnesses and they were there either to lend support or draw energy from a ceremony everyone seemed to like. It was written by Betty Dederich and explained, although we may choose to go separate ways, we can never truly be separated because we are all a part of the Synanon community and, like the branches of the Banyan tree, are all interconnected.

Max gave me a gift of a bottle of White Shoulders, which was the first toilet water I ever wore. Each couple shared thoughts. One woman read a poem to her husband of ten years. Max promised he would never take Elyse from me, and I believe he would never break that promise even if circumstances had put him in a position to do so. I'm not certain why Max changed partners. I didn't explore his deeper feelings then, or later on. I was swept up in the turbulent emotions that made me feel alive. I understood so little of deep commitment I mistook chaos and drama for more substantial emotion. I needed to be a good Synanon soldier, at the tip of the arrow, doing what we did with vigor. I was also at that magical three-year marker. I'd had my allotment of love—again. Time to let it go. Time to do some grieving. Time to start again.

After the ceremony I moved out of the house we'd shared and stayed with a woman whose husband had moved out of their living quarters. It was a time of utter chaos. My clothing was in one place, my bed in another and I went to work each day trying to carry on my life with some sense of routine. This lack of grounding was okay with me and served to fuel the energy it took to move into this upheaval we were all engaged in.

It was Chuck's voice that guided us through changing partners. Once again it is a voice I still have access to—I spent so much of my nineteen years in Synanon listening to it and studying it and allowing it to permeate my every membrane. This was a voice I heard in the deepest part of me as he was preparing the entire population to take part in this activity.

What's going on out there? Don't they understand, in the other facilities, what is happening here at the Home Place? Has anyone bothered to tell them what we're doing? Ending marriages on a high note. Not waiting until things get so bad couples hate each other. Ending relationships while there is still some good in the marriage. Starting new relationships on a high. Making love happen rather than waiting to be struck by lightning like some dumb teenager. This is the most important experiment Synanon's ever engaged in. Talk about changing the world. Curing dopefiends is chicken shit compared to this. And they're all out there waiting...making silly little dates...like teenagers...waiting for someone exactly like the one they were just with to come along. Dumb. Dumb. Let's get on with this. The idea is to mix it up. Hook up with people you might never have even thought of. The whole idea is if you love Synanon and cherish your new mate, love will follow. Love will result. You can make love happen. You can will it to happen. It's unbelievable. But goddammit, I have to do everything. You people all have your heads so far up your asses you've stopped working. Somebody get on the wire... Let's get this thing moving.

And somebody, following his manic orders, did indeed get on the wire and called everyone in the foundation to gather in major meeting rooms.

The rest is history, and history has perspective and context and texture and hindsight, and after so many years it might as well be fiction. It is also a history that contains a kaleidoscope of all the different marriages and relationships that existed at that time in Synanon. Older men and women, in their fifties and sixties, long married found it impossible to end their marriages and most left, including Chuck's own brother. Some people were single at the time, and it was an opportunity for them to start new relationships with perhaps greater ease than they had anticipated. Other marriages were in a down slope, and so this movement was accepted as a timely out. Some simply could not fathom this kind of invasion and left Synanon. And some suffered overwhelming loss and conflict over having to make the choice of allegiance to either Synanon or spouse, ultimately succumbing to their faith that Chuck knew what was best.

The evening that resulted in the establishment of hundreds of new couples began apprehensively when the instant communication network, the wire, summoned everyone to the Stew Temple in Tomales Bay and other gathering places in other facilities. The wire was almost a euphemism for Chuck or for the official word. It was not a free press and everything that flowed over the airwaves either originated from the source or was approved by Chuck or his office. Max had already hooked up with Pamela and they are still married today, as are a surprising number of those original changing partners unions. My emotions were not linear. I hadn't simply lost a husband who married another woman. I was completely caught up in the "experiment," the notion we could as a community "make love happen." The idea we, as a group, could accomplish the impossible held me captive those long years ago. It was about accessing that communal power when I, alone, felt powerless.

The air was chilly on that fall evening, and the large tin building was cold and dark. Walking through the coat-stacked vestibule, into the large gathering space, I spotted Jan standing in the middle of the room speaking into a microphone hanging from the ceiling. I have never been able to figure out what brought this tall, thin, quiet woman to the center of this cacophony of activity. Teased mercilessly by her friends for our having to lip read in order to compensate for her terminal mumbling, she was a woman of few words, choosing them with great care rather than spitting them out in the staccato fashion so admired in Synanon. And she was not prone to aggressively taking center stage. But there she was, like a grand slave auctioneer, matching couples within the Tomales Bay facility, and, by using the wire, hooking up people in Central California, San Francisco and Tomales Bay when necessary.

She was wearing an old pair of blue overalls that hung loosely over a faded cotton turtleneck, her brownish/orange hiking boots poking out from frayed cuffs. To ward off the chill she had on an oversized plaid flannel shirt. Her head was shorn like everyone else's, except Jan's fine straight hair poked out in different lengths refusing to submit to the quarter-inch cut we all sported. Perhaps she chose to play this role because it seemed like the only safe haven. With everyone so preoccupied with his or her own survival, her single status was ignored, and when the evening ended she remained unattached.

"Has Tom Blair hooked up with anyone yet? Jane is interested in him. Where is Tom? Tom! There you are. What about Janice?"

"Janice's okay. Yeah. I'll go with Janice."

"Where is Janice anyway? Does anyone know? In her room? What's she doing in her room? Can someone go and get her? Who will go and get her? Sue? Great. Okay. Janice and Tom are an item. Next."

People were sitting everywhere, in the big upholstered chairs that formed a neat circle, on the tables in front of the chairs, on folding chairs around the walls and all over the floor. It was too anonymous for me. Several men had inquired about me during the couple of days between my separation ceremony and this particular evening, inquiries that had come to me through various messengers, since for all of our electronic wizardry, telephones were scarce except

90

in the business areas and the homes of big shots.

"Alice, what about Jon? He's interested in you."

"No, absolutely not," came straight out of my gut. Thank God there were small residuals of intuition when I needed them. It seems that a fair number of pretty unstable men thought I would be an amazing catch. I also rejected some truly decent ones whose value I was as yet unable to recognize.

The energy in the large room was too charged with both anticipation and silent stories of fear and grief. I felt a need to flee. I decided what was needed was some ceremony. That was it. Ceremony. That was the role I chose for myself in this drama. I would find some candles and try to dignify what was going on with an improved atmosphere. On my way through the vestibule to find candles (candles—what was I thinking?), the phone rang, and as I have come to believe there are few accidents, my fate was to be directed by that phone call.

"Hello, Alice speaking."

"Oh, hello, Alice, this is Marvin Potter." He was, at the time of that call, with his new mate and had probably been called and told about the gathering in the Stew Temple. In the official voice of an executive committee member he asked, "How are things over there?"

"Well, things are certainly popping, but it's pretty chaotic, so I'm looking for some candles and stuff to try to bring some ceremony to what's going on." Why had I said that? Of all possibilities, why that? Was I looking for approval for my ability to enhance the celebrations?

He burst out laughing, not only because of the idiocy of my statement, but because this particular man thought candles in any situation were nothing more than a frivolous waste of time. Then regaining his composure, he hesitated as the thought occurred to him his new mate's ex-husband was still single. "Alice, have you hooked up yet?"

"No."

"What about Tony?" he asked.

My emotions settled down. Tony. Yes. This could work. Tony had been married to someone like me, someone close to my age, with a similar background. If this woman, a peer of mine, had been happy with Tony, had had a child with Tony, it could work for me. After all, this followed the totally unreasonable reasoning I had invented during this process—that if I knew and liked the wife, it followed that I could marry the husband. Tony was a "big shot," an old timer, practically a legend. He occupied a status that could perhaps afford me protection from the haphazard and quixotic hands of leadership, and protection is something I was always looking for in every relationship.

Marvin was clear in his next instruction. "Stay right where you are in the vestibule of the Stew Temple, and I'll come over to drive you down to Tony's house."

A NOT SO WILD WALK

Tony was an "old-timer dopefiend." Until changing partners, I had little interest in a romance with anyone from this group. The men in my life have all been nice guys, in general slow to anger, reasonable and sort of old-fashioned—holding car doors open and such. Guys who had really thrown all their cards in the air frightened me. They'd gone to the edge once and could do it again. Too scary for me. But this was changing partners. We weren't throwing everything in the air, but almost. It was a time for new risks.

For the next couple of months I was to have two brief encounters with old-timer dopefiends, the guys Chuck told us "built the place you live in" and, at the same time, called "dinosaurs," hopelessly incapable of understanding the growth of Synanon beyond a drug rehab program. He said dopefiends were imprisoned in character-disordered ways of thinking. Chuck called all addicts character disorders, which is simply not true. Some drug addicts and alcoholics are and some are not, just as some are criminals and some are people who never committed crimes. Chuck's sweeping generalizations were simplistic, and unfortunately many of the people who came for help believed what he told them about themselves: like the fact all dopefiends owed their lives to him; if not for Synanon and thus Chuck, they would be dead. That is just as simplistic. To be sure Synanon helped many addicts, but greater numbers left only to use drugs again. Those who stayed and became sober did so because they wanted to and worked hard at it. Synanon helped, but each newcomer did his own personal work, and each deserved to own his triumph.

Tomales Bay had three properties, The Bay property which overlooked Tomales Bay, The Ranch, which was the largest in terms of population and where the Stew Temple was located, and Walker Creek, which was the most remote. All of these properties were way out in the country, off well-traveled roads surrounded by rolling hills of green or yellow, depending on the time of year. The Walker Creek Property, where I was headed with Marvin, was five miles from the Ranch and one mile in from the main road, and then there was a smaller settlement of houses with no central meeting rooms, another half mile away called Walker II. Tony was in his small house on this farthest property, Walker II, hiding out. He and his wife, ex-wife now, had been one of the first couples in Tomales Bay to have their separation ceremony and he had reluctantly trailed her lead. To be sure their marriage was scarred and more tired than it might have been for their ages and time together, but Tony had not been ready to cash it in, and he was far less convinced than his wife that "The Old Man" was serious in his ramblings. Tony had been around for a long time and had figured out ways of sliding through the cracks when he wanted to avoid compliance. And it wasn't just the big things. He had trouble with all the new disciplines, often finding midnight, at the last possible moment, the only time to complete his aerobic exercise requirements.

Tony did not want to subject himself to this way of pairing. It seemed ridiculous to him. He figured if he just stayed in his house, through this particular night, maybe it would all go away. Maybe he would wake up in the morning and Chuck would announce that everyone who had gotten together the night before had to stay together, but everyone else was on their own. Anything was possible. "The Old Man" changed his mind as often as he changed his socks.

Marvin had an interest in getting Tony matched because he was with Tony's wife and didn't want her worrying about her former husband's well-being. Marvin's ex-wife had changed partners, and now if Tony would get happily engaged, Marvin would be free to develop his own relationship without concern about former mates who would be on their own to make love happen. I suppose it could be said his interest in this relationship between Tony and me grew from a sense of enlightened self-interest.

During that car ride, my head took flight with thoughts of newness. There was the anticipation of a safe entry into an unknown and somewhat dangerous world. A world of tattoos and fractured English and warmth and sympathy for broken people I only dimly understood. A world filled with a history of Synanon romanticized into mythical proportion. Tony and his peers, old-timers, the *dopefiends* who had lived in Synanon since its beginnings, held status filled with the duplicity that was so much a part of every aspect of Synanon. We were often reminded, when critical of one of them, that they had built the place eating substandard donated food and wearing ill-sized donated clothing during the early, lean years. They made the sacrifices that built Synanon into what it was at the time all of us, especially squares, came around. Over and over we were told Synanon had been built on the energy of their conversions, on the personal changes made by these early dopefiends one day at a time. They were the heroes.

They were also the *dinosaurs*. People who couldn't learn anything new. People who were stuck back there in the old Synanon: the Synanon that was merely a program. In the new Synanon— *Synanon the social movement*—they were lost, useless. This rhetoric swung back and forth with Chuck gaming individuals like Tony and discussed and lectured in the founder's monologues about the changing Synanon. It was never clear whether or not Chuck loved or despised this group of people. I suspect he did both. I know he used them shamelessly.

Many *square* women like myself had tumbled into this *dopefiend* world filled with men who were newcomers, newly in Synanon and barely removed from their use of drugs. Such young men represented an image of danger and some of these women thought of them as having greater sensitivity than the conventional men we knew. Tony was such a person, and I reasoned this would be a way for me to step into this world with a certain degree of safety, because he had been in Synanon for many years and had been married to someone with whom I easily identified. I also had visions of a new guide, ever hopeful for the ultimate protector, and perhaps Tony, who knew the ropes of Synanon better than most, could help protect me from difficulties that lurked everywhere.

But mostly, consistent with that time in my life, I was opening to the thought of something new. New was always easy for me. I loved starting a new job, making a new friend, entering names into a new address book, beginning a new knitting project, making a new marriage. They were all the same. A clean slate. A chance to do better—to do right—to not get enmeshed in messes I didn't know how to get out of. Newness came with promises, the promise to always use pencil in the address book; the promise to never say words in anger to a mate; the promise to not get my feelings hurt by a new friend; the promise to knit evenly and tie all my ends neatly; the promise to not get behind in whatever work I was doing. Promises that would all be broken in small or large ways with the passage of time.

The small house was dark when I entered. Tony knew I was coming, and although he greeted me with affection I felt I was entering a place of confusion. It was cool out, but the air in the house hung over us as if he'd been hiding in it for weeks. He was dressed in sweats, and a slight stubble covered his face. Furniture was in place, but pillows were askew and empty glasses filled the small sink. I looked deeply into this face which had been so handsome in its youth and was struck by how much it had aged, and how little of those early good looks could be seen under the weight of his sagging skin.

We talked for hours. His relief at having me delivered to his door was palpable.

"I have always admired you. You know how I felt about Eileen when I was married to her and I see many of the things I loved about her in you. I know how crazy I am, even though I've been here for over fifteen years, and I've always tried to surround myself with squares—kind of a balance. Not that uptight squares can't learn a thing or two from me. Ha."

He was worried about how people were handling the changing partners dictum. He had become practically undone by it and assumed he was not alone. What he didn't say was he had been immobilized by the command and simply gotten into bed and pulled the covers up so to speak.

"I think there are a lot of people really messed up. You should have been there tonight, Tony, it was a madhouse in the Stew Temple. I mean…people were hooking up left and right, people who hardly knew one another, just because…well just because they were afraid if they waited too much longer there wouldn't be anyone left. I don't know what I would have done if I hadn't just happened to pick up the phone at that moment."

"Do you think we should go over to the Ranch? Do you think there are people who need being taken care of? I feel like I should go and at least take a look."

And as quickly as he'd tapped into his "people business skills," he switched the conversation back to this new relationship and how excited he was about starting one with me, painting pictures of great intimacy and affection. I think Tony couldn't go to the Ranch because he was afraid the fact he'd been absent during the main event would be noted, and any repercussions were possible because of that.

In the earliest hours of the morning we got into bed and made love with the ease that all firsts have for me. For I was willing to present an openness that would tomorrow recede to a safer place.

We were in bed when his phone rang. After a brief hesitation, a shadow of fear hooded Tony's eyes, and he said, wearing the concern of an elder, "I'd better answer it."

His blood was pulsing. God only knew what was on the other end of that telephone. After all, he had indeed been hiding out in this small house, terrified he could become the subject of some wild whim of Chuck's. He could be ordered to mate with some person, a choice made either out of Chuck's largess or his twisted need to control. A choice made either out of Chuck's loyalty to an old-timer or out of his hostility toward him. And he knew had Chuck's attention come his way, had be been "chosen" for someone, he would have had to obey. He would have had no choice. He knew he was taking a big chance hiding out as he did, but he had hoped he would be overlooked. Now he feared word had gotten out he had not been around last night. That he had not been in the Stew room where he should have been. That he was still single.

What an asshole that Tony is. Did you know that he was hiding out in his house the entire time all hell was breaking loose in Tomales Bay? Just like a goddamned dopefiend. You can never count on them when you need them. Of course, he wouldn't be out there making sure things did not get out of hand. Of course, he would not be at the tip of the arrow leading the movement. Of course, he would just hide out, worrying about his own selfish dopefiend ass. Worrying about himself, of course. I can't be everywhere at once and, of course, I can't rely on the very people whose lives I saved to be there when I need them…biting the hand that feeds them. They're useless.

This imagined diatribe of Chuck's, similar to others directed at Tony over the years, must surely have played out in his head as he walked to the phone. Just as surely as he knew without doubt whatever hand Chuck dealt, he would play. He owed everything he had to this man who was becoming stranger and stranger, but one word from the founder about the person Tony had been before his life had been saved, one reminder about the person who had abandoned one whole set of family—wife, children, the works— and Tony would have been his.

Tony's demeanor carried into his voice, as he mumbled almost incoherently into the phone. I heard my name mentioned, and then a lot of silence, and then some more mumbling. I got dressed.

I soon found out Tony was on the phone with a tall, lank, redhead, Joan, one of those women who marched for causes and had a need to wear her personal philosophies like a neon light. She was one of those women who was always certain about what others should do, who others should be married to, where others should live, what others deserved or didn't deserve. She assaulted you with her views, which she presented as comfortably as a handshake. The worst part is that back then I imitated Joan and others like her in positions of power.

"Hello. Oh, hello Joan." There was a silence, as she explained to him Chuck's niece hadn't hooked up the night before and was interested in being with him.

Joan persuaded, "You're not just anybody, Tony. And we're talking about a Dederich. You should be with her. You've got to think about what's best for Synanon. Come on down to the Home Place. Everyone is very excited about having you with us."

I walked into the room where the phone was as he was hanging up.

"They want me to drive down to the Home Place to be with Chuck's niece."

He could have told her no, but I guess he was too scared. It must have felt like an order—so full of Dederiches and all. What if Chuck found out he had said no to his niece. Tony did not need any more of "The Old Man's" hostility.

My first reaction was horror. This couldn't possibly be what changing partners was about—ripping people apart after a few hours together—but I also saw this man had become completely deflated and had seen no way to simply tell Joan although he'd love to be with the young woman, he'd already hooked up. So sorry.

"Listen Tony," I sympathetically explained, "you do what you think is best. I understand completely."

"Gee, I feel just awful. I really want to stay right where I am, but they want me to come to the Home Place. I just don't see how I can say no."

"Tony, stop worrying. I really do understand. You should go. I'm just fine."

Possibly this acquiescence came from an inexplicable longing to please, but mostly I got the message that in the staunchly authoritarian hierarchy that was Synanon, it had been deemed I was a less-desirable mate for Tony than this other woman, or her lack of attachment was a more urgent priority. As a member of the Dederich family it was imperative her wish be honored, regardless of mitigating circumstances. It was a rejection, a statement of my lack of significance I felt powerless to attack, and so I absorbed it into an acquiescence I translated as proof of commitment and loyalty. I was confused about the difference between acquiescence and loyalty for most of the years I lived in Synanon. I also experienced a certain comfort in folding into that hierarchal structure at the hand of the mixers. I couldn't have lived in such a system otherwise.

And it is only now, so many years later, as I lie next to Jerry in bed holding hands and talking playfully towards bursts of laughter as one of us spins a shared reality inside-out, that I realize how weak my personal boundaries were.

Before Tony took off by car for the Home Place, which would take him the better part of a day, he wanted to find a game for us. It was customary to make important decisions public since Synanon was the third party in all relationships, but in this case, since Tony had practically been summoned by "the Vatican," it was done more out of consideration for my feelings. He wanted me to have an opportunity to say what I might not say out of a game. We drove over to the ranch property where a game had been bubbling for hours making available a place for people who needed a group to talk to. Vinnie, whom I was to be with briefly, was in that game.

Vinnie was not happy about changing partners. He had come to Synanon for the program. He liked rehabilitating drug addicts, and all this social movement, living experiment garbage that Chuck talked about meant nothing to him. He'd been a dopefiend and found help, promise, encouragement and hope from people like himself who had stopped using drugs before he had. He would work at whatever job was given him, but his purpose in being in Synanon was to pass on what he knew to the people who came after. The people business. The magic of Synanon was in the hope one addict gave the next hopeless person who walked through the door. The same hope that had gotten my attention. If these people could so dramatically change, then I could change too.

Someone in the game suggested since Vinnie was single, and I was once again single, we could get together. Vinnie said fine. I said fine, and we were together for a few short weeks. Vinnie didn't even pretend to try. I felt pretty awful during the time we were together because it was the first time I'd been with a man who really didn't want me, and my response was to see myself in a distorted fashion. I felt ugly and gnomish—almost disfigured—and was surprised when

I looked in a mirror that I still looked like myself. He couldn't "make love happen" and planned to secretly meet his ex-wife so they could talk about what to do. He was found out and Chuck reamed his ass in a public game.

He elaborated on the theme, "This is payback time and you scum bag dopefiends owe me."

Vinnie was shunned, even by people who shared his feelings of ambiguity about *Synanon the social movement*, as well as the loss of a loved one. Not long after, he left Synanon. His wife stayed, and the instant Vinnie was gone he became "the enemy," a splittee, even after fifteen years of residency, having been a tribe leader, department head and director. He had been a valuable member of the Synanon community for many years, but once in Chuck's disfavor he was easily shunned. When he left people said, as they inevitably did, something like, "Good riddance, just more deadwood out of the way."

JOHN

I had changed partners with Tony and then with Vinnie and then I was single. Jerry had hooked up with someone, so he was out of the picture. John was my next partner and I was to be with him for almost three years, but during the period of time I was single after Vinnie, he was still married to Kimberly. He and Kimberly had been told by Chuck they did not have to change partners because Kimberly had just had a mastectomy. I heard Chuck tell her she was like a daughter to him and he would take care of her. They were moved into the best housing—a three-bedroom double-wide mobile home—and John was given a job as Chuck's stockbroker and set up in a beautiful office at the Home Place where Chuck lived.

John was a guy who had a hard time connecting. He had an odd combination of traits—he was funny as all hell, a stand-up comedian who wrote and delivered his own material like a pro. He could do anything with his hands—draw, paint, fix things. We were once on a trip and the entire seat of his pants split, not only in the seam but into the actual seat itself. He took the pants apart and, with only a needle and thread, sewed them back together so you couldn't see where the tear was. He was smart and articulate and so intense the veins and sinew in his neck jutted. As much as you'd think these characteristics would connect him to people and in spite of the fact that people enjoyed his company, he remained angry and alienated, giving off the feeling that something long ago had really pissed him off, but he was too manly to dwell on such things.

He and Kimberly had had a rocky romance and marriage until Kimberly's illness released something in him. We were a youthful population. The vast majority of us were in our late-twenties to mid-thirties, so as a group we had not dealt with much in the way of life-threatening illness. There had been a couple of cases of cancer, but mostly in older or middle-aged residents. For John, dealing with Kimberly's cancer awakened a very important part of him. From the moment he saw the yellow liquid squirt out of her breast he changed, a vein of compassion was struck, and he became devoted to her care. He bathed her scar, tapping into a reserve of tenderness and concern that nourished his soul as much as it nourished her. He felt their dispensation was well deserved and didn't doubt for one minute Chuck would allow them to stay together. He was being cradled in the net we all knew would be there for us. He wasn't paying much attention to changing partners.

In December, 1996 I was diagnosed with breast cancer. It takes a while to understand the diagnosis of breast cancer is not a death sentence. It takes time to wade through terrifying statistics until you teach your brain that statistics in and of themselves are meaningless.

I'm lying in bed reading one of my many cancer books after my surgery. Jerry is in the family room doing his multi-media thing. He has the TV tuned to a basketball game with the sound off. He is listening to a radio broadcast of that same game as he goes through his pile of mail—the newspaper, *Popular Science* magazine and two thousand pieces of investment advice and information.

I yell from the bedroom, "Jerry one half of all the women diagnosed with breast cancer will be dead within ten years."

He slowly walks to the doorway and slumps against the door frame. "Alice, you're killing me with these statistics. What women? Women from all over the world, third-world countries, the United States? What part of the United States? Women diagnosed when? Stage 0, Stage 1, Stage 2, Stage 3? Women treated, not treated?"

And he did this over and over and over again, every time I erupted with some poorly-stated statistic that must have been intended to inform me of something other than how to be terrified. He caught me every time I tripped and let me know time and again this was happening to the two of us and we'd figure it out together. My kids stopped everything, including long-planned holiday vacations, and came to hang out while I exclaimed over and over I couldn't believe I had cancer. Friends called and visited and waited with Jerry while I was in surgery. There was not much anyone could do except listen as I talked myself through the information and tried to sort out what was right for me. There is no way to measure what their support did for me, and the thought of not having had Jerry at my side during surgery, treatment and recovery, and as a partner to the many lifestyle decisions I've made since cancer, scares me much more than having cancer does. Knowing this, what happened next with John and Kimberly was, I realize now, unconscionable.

Not long after his original decision, Chuck told John he had to change partners. God knows why. There had been a couple of dispensations, and surely John and Kimberly could have made three. Everyone was ordered to change partners. There were to be no further exceptions. John worked directly for Chuck. He was set up like a king and had to pay back—do what we were doing. It wasn't a mistake or an oversight. Chuck told him directly. Kimberly was whisked away and paired with a man with whom she remained until her death several years ago. They left Synanon a couple of years after changing partners and I do not know much about their life together, but I certainly hope she received the care from him she most certainly deserved.

John was prodded and poked by his friends at the Home Place to choose a woman. All of this happened in the period of about twenty-four hours. In a daze, and with great reluctance, he chose me after hearing a list of all the available women—several times over. It was not my greatest moment, but I knew John to be a good, solid citizen and was excited at the chance to live at the Home Place. The Home Place, the name of any place Chuck and his wife lived, was always the center of Synanon. To be close to Chuck and all the action was not a bad reward for the trouble changing partners had given me thus far. I can't believe knowing the details of John's breakup I could have been thinking that. My head was full of such rot. I was so terribly out of it—grasping at everything and anything new, any distraction, never looking beneath the surface at the subtext. By this time my world had shrunk. I no longer read or listened to music. Going outside to movies was frowned upon and we didn't get many to watch in the community. We had little time for TV. My world was tiny and my head was filled with nothing but the sounds of Synanon.

Everyone supported Chuck's mandate that John and Kimberly change partners. I do not recall one person, in or out of games, commenting on how difficult a move that must have been considering the circumstances of Kimberly's cancer. John and I had a terrible time of it, and although there were many reasons why we could never have connected as I would have wanted, I never heard one single person suggest the reason John and I had so many problems building a relationship was because the foundation of that relationship was rotten to the core—Synanon magic, making love happen, cherishing your mate or not. It's sad John did not have it in him to tell Chuck to go fuck himself, that he would not leave Kimberly, and if they had to leave so be it. It's sad I was so lost I jumped into that quicksand and actually believed I could walk in it. But what Chuck did was mean and cruel, not simply another mandate to implement a new experiment, and was just one of a long string of abuses of his immense power.

It is so clear to me now. The power to tell others what they may or may not do in their personal lives is dangerous and can only lead to corruption.

JERRY

After almost three years, in August of 1980, I gave up on John and decided to move on. It was a very sad move for me and reminded me that once again I'd failed at building a long-term relationship. No matter what, I was unable to move a relationship past the three-year mark. An old sense of hopelessness returned at the thought of yet another failure. I was sad at having to leave the Home Place, because being a resident of that tiny community held such status and I was still awed at how different it was from other Synanon communities, how much more experimental and unified it was. Chuck was always present, and there was no confusion about what he wanted. In the other facilities there was always the disadvantage of distortions of information and mandates as they were interpreted by his directors. At the Home Place there was no such ambiguity. Chuck was clear on what he wanted and did not want. I was certain I would never have another opportunity to live so close to the center of Synanon. I was also relieved to be returning to Elyse in Marin County and closer to Jules who was in San Francisco, but mostly troubled I hadn't been able to make my "love match" to John work out.

The "love match" was a Synanon ceremony during which an executive officiated before a couple who promised to give commitment and fidelity a try for three years. One of the partners could end the relationship after three years, or the commitment could be renewed. This was a great invention for people who had problems with forever promises and gave many couples who would otherwise have avoided a committed relationship a chance at it. I grieved the end of this relationship as I had grieved the end of most of the others.

Today I am pleased that John and I were love matched and not actually married. Because we were not legally married, I don't have to count him as a husband if I don't want to. Sometimes it matters to me that I was married five times, so I just cut John off the list to make it four. There, that feels so much better.

At the same time I ended my relationship with John at the Home Place in Central California, Jerry, who was living in Marin

County, was also ending a love match. He learned I was single, and, God bless his security, made another attempt to ask for my hand. As soon as he was told I was open to the idea of a relationship with him, he wrote me a note that revealed so much of who he is. The note is buried in my basement in a box of notebooks I have yet to find. It was short, thoughtfully composed, warm and loving yet restrained. He told me in the note he was excited about my coming to Tomales Bay. He told me how he used to watch me back in the early seventies when I worked in the school in Oakland. He described how I looked to him back then. It was a lovely note, filled with more positive attention than I'd received in a long time. I was so tired of not being adored I said yes, only suspecting how ready I was for what he had to give me. Before I moved away from the Home Place a huge, shiny, white box arrived for me. Friends gathered around a dining room table as I opened one box after another, smaller and smaller, finally unwrapping a tiny bottle of perfume. Real perfume. My first bottle of real perfume—ever. And I loved what was the beginning of what was to be one gift and surprise after another.

I took a long ride in an old greyhound bus Synanon owned called the Synacruiser, and when I arrived in Tomales Bay Jerry was waiting for me. He hugged me placing his hands in the small of my back and I felt great gentleness and warmth. He has two gestures he has repeated hundreds of times over the past eighteen years, and I get the same new feeling of awe every time he does them. One is to place his hand in that very same spot on my back as we walk, and the other is to take my hand, pull it to his lips, and gently kiss it as we drive, watch a movie or lie in bed reading.

I had always been attracted to Jerry. We first met in 1972 when he was about to end a relationship, and I was considering entering

108

into a relationship with a different man. Although I found Jerry attractive, I chose to date the other man because dating Jerry would have fractured an image I took very seriously. First, Jerry is almost three years younger than I, and that taboo fits way up there with taboos about women dating shorter men. I did grow up in the fifties, and I have certain pictures that can be modified only with great effort. These were the kinds of things I felt viscerally back then, I had no words for them but was vaguely troubled by the superficial nature of my reasoning. I was also of the opinion that Jerry was too similar to me. We were both Jewish, raised by similar kinds of people, if you weren't looking too closely, and could have met just about anywhere. This was not what my life was about. My life was about new landscapes, distant cultures, uncharted territory. I rejected Jerry for these reasons and more. I rejected Jerry because I was unable to bring him into focus. I had not yet found my center of gravity and was not yet able to accept the kind of love and decency of which he was capable.

It seems so much easier to talk about the problematic areas of my life than the ones that work. I guess this is true in general if you think about the kinds of songs written, movies produced and books on the shelves. Sadness, dysfunction, loss, greed, poverty and corruption gather larger audiences than smooth, predictable stories of nourishment and growth. Perhaps this is why it is difficult to translate my relationship with Jerry and the kind of anchor he has been for me.

When I was a young child I spent a great deal of time fantasizing about my lost father, but in those daydreams I never saw him buying me the things I wished for. I never saw him rescuing me from the anger of my mother. I never even pictured him doing things with me. I imagined he watched me from heaven and his love rained down upon me like the warm showers we took together when I was two- and three-years old. I suppose those imaginings provided me with some of that missing love. From the moment I met Jerry I felt as if that childhood fantasy had been realized. There were no thunderbolts. There were no great insights. But as with all change that is substantive, there was a gradual shifting of the ground beneath me, of attitudes and expectations, and from day one I knew this was to be an experience different from any I had ever known.

It would be dishonest of me to convey that Jerry and I stepped into marital bliss from minute one, although a calm and satisfying companionship began almost immediately. I had a partner, someone who was interested in my life in its entirety and someone who was willing to share his with me. This had a soothing effect. But I am who I am, and that young woman—with a harsh tongue, a propensity toward impatience, quick to express anger—did not die an easy death. Jerry was not fond of these characteristics, and I was impatient with his inability to accept them or even to acknowledge them when they reared their multiple heads. He just withdrew in the slow and steady way he did everything else.

Another major problem we had occurred when our marriage reached the three-year mark. In spite of the fact that I had an awareness that the three year anniversary held the potential for problems and viewed the approaching period like a hunter about to be attacked from behind, I still managed to try to sabotage the relationship. My internal program was still in place, three years was all I got, then I had to give it up, just as I had to give up my father after receiving three years of his love. It is no coincidence all of my marriages lasted for three years, even though they each ended quite differently. It was becoming difficult to ignore the pattern. And to

110

prove how insidious this pattern was, I was separated from both of my children during the third year of their lives. I missed the day-to-day development of both of my little girls when they were the same age I was when I lost my father. This had been an experience filled with so much pain and was so deeply embedded in me that even as an adult I kept reliving it.

When Jerry and I were in our third year of marriage, I told him that my sex drive had dwindled and that I found myself having little interest. It was true. I wasn't making it up. I had almost no interest in sex. I now know this is a lethal pronouncement to most men whose sense of power and adequacy is intimately tied to their ability to perform and provide. Jerry would always be able to provide, but I poked a giant hole in his feeling of adequacy by telling him I was no longer interested in sex, especially so early in our marriage. There was no dialogue about this, it came in the form of a pronouncement, with the caveat he should not take it seriously, for if he initiated sex, I would eventually respond. This went on for several months. I gamed the issue so the entire community could be witness to Jerry's growing feelings of impotence, and to add insult, I expressed impatience that he should feel much of anything. It's not as if I refused to have sex. It was just mostly up to him right now.

Fortunately I was forty-one years old by this time, and as Jerry withdrew more and more from me, initiating sex less frequently, I realized exactly where I was heading and was able to save myself from immolation. This is a technique that is foolproof, but one that, to this day, slips in and out of my grasp like melting ice.

When I realized I was killing this relationship which was only three years old, I wrestled with possible solutions. I really did not feel particularly seductive, so play-acting was not an option. How was I to take this stiff body and transform it into vampish flexibility?

How was I to bring our sexual relationship back to normal? That was a giant step and I needed to come up with a baby step. When I did, it was exquisitely simple.

Shortly before noon each day, Jerry and I met by the big fireplace in the Home Place lodge. There we stood, in winter before the fire that heated our backs, and in summer we sat on the cool hearth waiting for twelve o'clock sharp when the men would sit together and the women did likewise. On the day of my breakthrough, I moved close to Jerry and motioned I had something to whisper to him.

"Let's make sure we go home early tonight. Let's have a romantic date, okay?"

It was that simple. His chest puffed and testosterone began coursing through his body landing smack in the center of his brain which then signaled that everything was back to normal. He spent the day assured that I was back, looking forward to a heavenly evening. That night he took the initiative and although I didn't return immediately to my former sexual self, gradually things did return to normal. It was all about restoring his confidence in us, which I had been slowly chipping at. I have tried to hold on to this notion as other relationship issues, with Jerry, my children and friends, come to my attention: finding small ways to begin the repair is the only way toward healing that is substantial. Finding that small way is not as easy at it might seem, and I too often find myself looking at the problem in its entirety which serves only to keep me immobilized.

It is fashionable to say no marriage is perfect, and certainly Jerry and I have glitches and misunderstandings, and inconsiderations that rankle from time to time. It is also probable outsiders viewing us notice failings in the way we relate owing to personality flaws I am not aware of. But I think our marriage is as near perfection as is possible. Consider that we have paid our dues in our other relationships and learned from them. This is one way of doing it. Each year I am surprised by some aspect of the marriage I never even considered a possibility for me. Jerry goes out to our deck with the mobile phone while I am sitting on the sofa reading. I know he was talking to Julie, but an hour has passed and I assume he has called someone else and is probably deep into a business or financial conversation. I walk onto the deck into what has now become night and whisper, "Who are you talking to?"

"Jules," he mouths back at me. I stand quietly inside the open door and listen.

"Julie, as a man, I can tell you guys just don't get these things until they are much older. When I was Tim's age, I wouldn't have known what you are talking about. Tim is a sweet guy, but he's got to work out the situation with his folks before he can...."

Jerry and Jules had been discussing the breakup of her relationship for over an hour. He takes the lives of these daughters of ours as seriously as he takes mine. A surprise gift, way beyond my expectation that he merely support me in my efforts with them. I wouldn't dream of asking for more, which is why I am so consistently surprised by Jerry who always gives more than is expected.

Just as my mother's anger brought my very cells to their knees when I was growing up, Jerry's love has slowly penetrated my skin working its way into those very same cells helping them to slowly rise to their feet.

There is another side to Jerry, and I hope never to be on the other end of a business negotiation with him because he is calmly but psychotically tenacious. The people in our office scratch their heads and roll their eyes in amazement. He's doing it again. It sounds like he's just talking normally, but once you catch on to what he's up to you can only feel sympathy for the person on the other end of the phone who everybody knows is going to cave long before Jerry is ready to give an inch. But being his wife is the greatest. Because he truly loves women, he tries—even when it is difficult—to understand us, and although his eye wanders as testosterone surges and aging threatens in the way that it does in men, he comprehends the enormous hurt infidelity inflicts. I have long since decided I would forgive if those hormones ever got the better of him, but I think I decided that because in my heart I doubt he would ever be unfaithful to me.

Jerry and I made it through my three-year wall which was in 1983. He was, as always, patient and thoughtful as I went through other personal changes as we moved into the fourth and fifth years of our marriage. In Synanon, our marriage was stable and we were partners in every way, but there were important conversations we never had, conversations about changes we were witness to that gave us pause. We remained fearful of "the third party" Synanon, and its power to insinuate itself into relationships, even to demand they end. But emotionally we were becoming more and more tied to one another and as a result developed a root system stronger than that of the community, which was beginning to crumble. My primary allegiance gradually moved from vision and dream and philosophy to this person who was making such a quiet yet huge impact upon my life.

We started a business one year after we left Synanon. Jerry was still working for Synanon, and it was a struggle to extricate him from the sense of loyalty and responsibility that lingered even after he realized the management of Synanon felt no loyalty to him, other than to compensate him for the sales he accrued. He felt a deep sense of responsibility to continue to do his share, and it took a year of persuasion by me and some of our friends to get him to make the move to go it on his own. Our business competes with the remnants of the Synanon business, but there's a big cake out there and enough buyers for us all to make a decent living selling companies things to print their names on. All I can say is that Jerry is good, really good, and the business is a small gem of success. We worked side by side for the first three years and with each month, my confidence shrunk in the shadow of his competence. He knew so much and I knew so little; I hadn't talent, aptitude or interest in learning this industry. He gave me complete support in cutting back hours to devote more time to writing, and the only resistance I had to face was my own. It is harder to look at hidden strengths and desires than hidden weaknesses. We are more afraid of what it is possible to accomplish than what we might fail at. Jerry and I try to guide each other toward the pursuit of those hidden strengths.

Jerry is a problem solver, which is how he came to love my kids. Kids present problems and Jerry feels compelled to find solutions. Jules has a full time dad, Brian, whom she adores and who adores her. Jerry is right in there loving and helping and thinking about her, but the emotional expression of their bond is a quiet one. Jerry was Elyse's second dad every day since she was thirteen, giving directly to her and running interference when I was unfair. They have a unique relationship.

Some of the reasons Jerry came to Synanon are the same as mine, and some are different. He was unattached—responsible to or for no one but himself—so he does not share my sense of guilt over abandoning relationships, although he does feel we have a lot to make up to the kids. Jerry also never used drugs, and one of the main reasons he moved into Synanon was because making decisions was difficult for him. He was faced with making a choice between two highly desirable jobs, and he chose to move into Synanon because it was easier. On the surface this does not seem like much of a problem, but dealing with choices, especially choices of equal promise immobilizes Jerry. Our marriage has been good for this. I tend to be very decisive and I also tend to probe, which he finds helpful.

Mother Theresa said that none of us can do great things, but we can do small things with great love. I think I began to understand this when I found Jerry. The grandiose vision that Synanon was saving the world began to fade. Principle over personality began to feel like a poor excuse for the inability to have great love. Jerry's love became both an anchor that created the desire for roots sturdier than the ones I was growing in Synanon, and it served to fill me up to the point that my own great love began to overflow.

PART III
THE DARK SIDE

CHUCK

Those of us who were under Chuck's spell for ten, twenty, even thirty years find it difficult to agree about who he was, and we have little emotional distance regarding him. Because he is so controversial, placing him at the center of the dark side of Synanon has been difficult. How many more people will I turn against me by suggesting Synanon's shadows flow directly from Chuck? We who lived in Synanon for decades were deeply committed to sharing responsibility for all that happened. "Let me first and always examine myself" was an oft-repeated line of the Synanon prayer, and although we might point a finger in the game we would invariably end up with fingers pointed back at us. What part did we play in any particular event, or what might we have done to prevent a wrong from happening?

Chuck was the tether, the center, the pivot of Synanon. To talk about darkness without talking about Chuck won't work. Perhaps questions about him rather than answers will serve me better in trying to move into an understanding his role in violence and criminal activity.

Was Chuck a brilliant visionary or was he a con man? Did he truly believe in the vision of an integrated community where people would be treated well and each man's abilities respected? Did he truly believe in the integrity of the human spirit, and everyone's right to a second chance and supportive community within which to set life on a healthy course? Did he build a system wherein people were enabled to do right and disabled from doing wrong? Or was he a clever con artist who seized upon a population of people so dependent and confused he was able to use this vision as a hook to keep them long after they were clean and sober? Was he just clever enough to assess young people (squares like me) who came to visit Synanon to lend support and became inspired by the alternative lifestyle? Did he seize the opportunity by dishing out a philosophy of idealism that would inspire us to want to devote our skills to a world over which he could have complete control?

Was his immense energy during the building years the result of inspired vision, dedication, love and generosity, or was it simply an effect of his manic depressive disease? Did he really put in hour after hour, making us all feel small compared to his intense persistence, building Synanon and then intentionally retreat into the background to watch how we handled the day-to-day running of the place without him? Or did he go on and on, seemingly without sleep, dealing with every single aspect of Synanon until he dropped into a hidden exhausted depression the general population knew nothing about? There was a cycle that was repeated over and over. After his quiet period, he would reappear with a flourish telling us everything was all "fucked up" and he would go at it again, setting things right. Was this cycle simply the result of his mental disorder, or was he truly building Synanon then backing off to see how well we could handle things on our own?

Internal rules were always rigid. Borrowing a stamp was dealt with as theft, and minor infractions of the many "small r rules" of Synanon were often given a heavy hand. We were very careful about presenting a lawful and conservative face. We didn't allow our teenagers to have sex until they were of age, and living together without a marriage commitment was frowned upon. Chuck talked about "Mrs. Grundy"—the average American who donated money to us and bought our promotional items and how we had to please her. But did he also see himself and Synanon as above or outside the law? There were many small, seemingly insignificant instances in the early days when we, Synanon, took the law into our own hands as when we went after residents who split with stolen items or stood above the law regarding any kind of government compliance concerning the management of our facilities. It also seems we invented creative ways of keeping books because as Chuck said over and over, we were doing God's work.

Exactly what role did Chuck play in the lawlessness and criminal behavior we now know about? What did he know about our accounting practices that ultimately led the IRS to virtually close us down with their demand for back taxes? How much of the violence did he know about, and how much did he direct either through subtlety or direct orders to those he trusted never to tell? Did he know a rattlesnake was placed in the mailbox of a lawyer who had just won a kidnapping case against Synanon? Did he order the beating of an ex-resident who challenged his authority? Did he know about the individual acts of violence that took place against neighbors, ex-residents and even people who lived in Synanon, or did he simply play a *Godfather* role speaking in euphemism? We all heard him order someone to… "bring me Morantz' (the rattlesnake lawyer) ear in a bottle," a command shouted during a session in which he waxed on all manner of subjects called "think table." He claimed anything said at think table fell under the category of freedom of speech just like in the game.

There were countless acts of violence and lawlessness committed by Synanon residents. I know about some of them, and I'm certain there are many more I do not know about. I believe everyone who lived in Synanon is completely responsible for all acts they

120

individually committed. I believe the people who stopped using drugs did so because they used the resources of Synanon, and they are one-hundred-percent responsible for their own conversions. I believe those of us who changed partners did so because we made the decision to do so. I believe the men who had vasectomies at Chuck's command must take personal responsibility for that act. But it is not quite that simple.

The two young men who placed the rattlesnake in the lawyer's mailbox were told to do so. They did not just decide of their own free will to find a virulent baby rattlesnake, check out a vehicle at the front desk (which was difficult to do under normal circumstances) and drive to Los Angeles to attack this lawyer who they most probably knew little about. There was a chain of command. One of the men was a violent drug addict who had come to Synanon for help not long before the incident. It would have been easy to tap into his short fuse so early into his rehabilitation. The other was still a teenager. There is a relationship here between the led and the leader that cannot be ignored.

The idea to change partners did not come from me. Chuck told us we all had to do this or leave Synanon. But I decided to do it rather than leave. I might have left as many others did, but I had little to go to and much to leave behind. Besides, I had bought into the notion that change was good and Chuck knew what was best for us.

We were told over and over we had powerful enemies who were after Chuck; Chuck must be protected. For those of us who loved Synanon there was little choice. For those who believed Chuck had saved their lives there was little choice. Even for those who made some separation between Chuck and Synanon, if Synanon was threatened in any way, there was no choice. Chuck, unlike many other gurus, was not divinely inspired; some deity's vision was not passed through him. He was the vision. He was divine. He was Synanon. If he declared something was good for Synanon, who were we to question it? He was synonymous with Synanon and Synanon was doing God's work.

Men gathered in groups to train in martial arts and the use of guns. Synanon purchased one-hundred-thousand dollars worth of guns and ammunition that were placed in gun lockers in every facility. Target practice became a hobby for some of us, but for others it was taken seriously. Many people, me included, bought guns, and there was a time when some officials wore loaded guns on their belts— even in games. Violence had crept into Synanon slowly, and we dared not question it because our very way of life was supposedly in grave danger.

It is most difficult to isolate Chuck and talk about him because he was such an integral part of all that was Synanon. Perhaps the subtle interplay of his leadership, his demand for obedience and his assumption of lawlessness can be best demonstrated through the story of Paul Runyon. But before I get to Paul, I need to talk about vasectomies.

VASECTOMIES

It was during my pregnancy with Elyse that Chuck began talking about childlessness. By this time, in 1975, more and more demands had been placed upon us; we had our two main rules, no drugs or physical violence, even though knocking down teenage delinquents had become an accepted routine practice no one seemed to question. We didn't smoke. We had to do mandatory aerobic exercise four times a week for twenty minutes. We were not allowed to eat sugar. And now, shortly before I was about to give birth to my second child, Chuck decided we would not be having any more children in Synanon.

This issue was gamed for months. Having our own children was too expensive, too many parents interfered with the experiment of raising children communally, and after Synanon's immense investment in a child, parents too often left with their kid. Chuck decided instead of trying to make the school work, we were going to address ourselves to taking care of the world's children. We were going to find the children no one wanted and raise them in Synanon; as always surrounding a mandate with a vision only a small-minded person could argue.

Several big shot couples who had already made the decision to be childless were the centerpieces for a series of public games we all listened to, and they extolled the virtues of not having children. One woman whose beauty was a defining element talked about not wanting her body wrecked, and there was the more popular view that having children took energy from the important work of Synanon—taking care of newcomers, raising money to continue our work, teaching our principles—which was a never ending pursuit. It was not so much a matter of personal sacrifice as it was a decision to simply devote more energy to the work of Synanon.

As always, Chuck's voice carried the most force. He not only painted the vision with a new slant on caring for the world's outcasts and surrounded himself with attractive supporters, but he reintroduced an old theme about men and children that went something like this: *Men don't care about kids. What man here can honestly say he thinks about his kids two times a week? What man can honestly tell me that he ever thinks about going over to the school? You go because your wives whine that you're not interested, they want you to take more interest in your offspring. You men who say you want kids have some kind of bullshit fantasy about seeing your own genetic offspring. Well, for most of you that would be too bad. You'd only be passing on the genes that got you into the messes that brought you to Synanon. The reason we started the school is because men don't want to be around their kids until they're adults, and you women mother-love them into sissies and punks if left to your own devices.*

There were a few small voices declaring these unwanted children we were going to take care of didn't exist, there weren't many adoptable children available, and we, a highly controversial community, were unlikely to be approved for adopting those who were. These voices of reality were muffled by Chuck along with the vocal group of women and men who had become spokespersons for the movement. These small voices were correct.

As usual some people packed up and left, riding off property in prearranged pick ups, they engineered lifts into town or simply walked down the road in the hope of hitchhiking to a bus station. Others at the upper range of childbearing age, in their mid- to late-thirties, talked themselves into believing having gone this long without reproducing was a sign raising children was not to be for them. Those of us with children were not particularly involved, except to wonder what we might have done had we been ten years younger and childless. And some people struggled with the concept even long after vasectomies were completed and reproduction was no longer an option in their present situations.

One of the saddest happenings of this period was what I have come to refer to simply as the abortions. Four women, in addition to Beatrice and I, were pregnant. Beatrice and I were way too far into our pregnancies to have abortions. Of the other four, three

124

were in their first trimester, and one was just beyond that. Three of them were in their mid-thirties and very much wanted to have their babies. The other was younger and has subsequently had a family. None of the three older women ever did have children. All four were told to have abortions to support childlessness and they all complied. A friend, many years later, referred to these abortions as yet another act of violence on her list of Synanon offenses. It was the first time I considered these abortions in terms of violence.

Meanwhile, Mary, Beatrice and I were tucked away in a small house called "the hatchery." Beatrice, a master of gallows humor, walked into the living room one day holding Tamara in the crook of one arm and looking down at her announced to Mary and me, "Why do I feel like I am holding a forbidden cigarette in my hand every time I look at Tamara?" It is no wonder, as I look back, that our children and their entry into the school was paid so little attention.

Chuck decided the way to accomplish childlessness was for every man who had been in Synanon for five years and was over eighteen to have a vasectomy. This meant a nineteen-year-old man who had come to live in Synanon with his parents when he was twelve would have to have a vasectomy or leave, as would a twenty-one-year-old who had come to Synanon for help at sixteen. All six resident doctors were trained to do the procedure by a local urologist, after the male doctors had their surgeries by the same urologist. Schedules were formalized and the medical facility was reorganized to convert examination rooms so they could be used to perform the operations.

Large areas were designated for the men's recuperation. Single beds were set up dormitory style complete with end tables, reading lamp, and TVs. Men were taken to these dorms after their surgery so they could rest for twenty-four hours under the care of volunteers and medical staff who would feed them and this allowed them to enjoy the time off they required. The event was transformed into yet another group process. Porno films were rented so the "clipped" men could see first-hand that things were still in working order.

I assisted Max as he did one surgery after another. I was certain I had the stomach for it and did fine after the first cut during which I had to quickly find a seat that I could land on as I put my head between my legs to avoid a faint. The sight of that small sharp knife cutting into the flesh of the first testicle remains clearly imprinted on the inside of my head, especially since the young man was twenty-one years old. But as with so much in Synanon, after the first rush of intuitive apprehension, I became a trouper, and plowed through one surgery after another until, as a group, we accomplished hundreds of vasectomies in one or two short days.

I have often wondered how it is the vasectomies, the sterilization of most of the men in Synanon, happened before changing partners. What hierarchy of values is represented by this chronology? Why would sterilization, a decision so finite, be easier than giving up a mate whom you could always reclaim down the road a bit? Why did Chuck demand all the men have vasectomies instead of the women getting their tubes tied? The procedure is easier on men, but Chuck was clearly a man's man, a macho, paternalistic, authority figure.

I think I get it now. Asking a population of women to sterilize themselves would not have flown. We are far too emotional about childbearing, and, the women's liberation movement notwithstanding, gestating human life is the greatest act of creativity on earth. And we own it. Men are not as connected to their reproductive function, are less defined by it, and they could assuage their doubts with the knowledge that vasectomies are sometimes reversible.

Vasectomies came prior to changing partners because giving up a mate was immediately painful; the tearing of a giant emotional bandage from sensitive skin. Giving up the ability to reproduce was a future consideration for most of the men. It had to be the men, for even in my Synanon stupor and under the veil of seven months of pregnancy, I distinctly remember asking myself if I would have stayed had I been younger and childless. I wondered whether I would have my tubes tied even after giving birth to two children and having no intention of any future pregnancies. Would I do something so finite and irreversible? What if something happened to one of my children? Would I be willing to give up the ability, so at the core of my identity, to bear a child? I was consciously grateful this was a decision I did not have to make.

PAUL RUNYON

Paul Runyon is a tall man with a Jimmy Stewart kind of awkwardness. He worked his way toward an accounting degree by working on cars and became a fine auto mechanic in the process. It was natural for him to take over as head of the automotive department in Synanon, watching over the fleet of vehicles Synanon owned. He also established a program that trained newcomers to work on cars. It was a strange picture, this tall, thin, chiseled man underneath cars, training newcomers—street people; dopefiends—rough, hopeless dead-enders with deeply-etched New York accents, cut-off syllables, slurred right-on, gotcha covered kinds of guys. Paul, who moved slowly and spoke calmly with reserve, loved these young men and he loved the work he was doing. Where else could he have combined his skills to such an end? He and his wife had formed a sort of small family with these young men, and the thought of these kids, as he saw them, being subjected to forced sterilization, which he believed should be a matter of individual conscience, was more than he could tolerate.

He had gamed the matter and talked to people he considered powerful in Synanon and realized regardless of their personal feelings, which were often in agreement with his, they were not going to challenge Chuck. Some actually told him they agreed with him, agreed it was both wrong and dangerous, but they owed "The Old Man" and would not challenge him. These were mostly men who had come before us, heroin addicts, many of whom had hurt parents, abandoned wives and children as their lives had spiraled downward. Chuck didn't let them forget their former lives, and much of the glue that held his army together was their accumulated guilt. Paul purposely avoided being in a game with Chuck because he was afraid the powerful man might persuade him to let go of his crusade. And he couldn't.

One morning, days before the vasectomies were scheduled, he took his motorcycle and some pocket change and headed for the authorities, who he hoped would be able to stop Chuck from having the surgeries performed. He went to the sheriff and the district attorney and the ACLU, but judicial time and Synanon time were of different dimension, and he couldn't get the legal machine to work fast enough. It would have taken six weeks before a hearing on the subject could be held, and many of the people he spoke to were not terribly alarmed that a group of addicts, many of whom had engaged in criminal behavior, were agreeing to the procedure. The vasectomies would go on as scheduled; several hundred men would be "clipped."

On the day of his motorcycle ride while Paul was in one of the offices he visited to try to get the operations stopped, someone from the office phoned the Synanon law department and during that phone call Paul was told not to come home. In an instant he became a splittee, an untouchable with a contagious disease—negativity.

Paul experienced a powerful internal push–pull regarding Synanon. He was rejected and ultimately excommunicated, but at the same time remained as blinded by the vision of Synanon as I. Even with this internal confusion, on January 11, 1977 shortly after he was told not to come home, in a letter he accused Chuck of finally taking complete leave of his senses and informed him that he, Paul, had "too much to lose to conform to mindless acceptance of every utterance you make with no discrimination attempted between the trivial and the monumental." In his letter he put forth several arguments the last of which was almost clairvoyant in its accuracy: "That it (vasectomies) further marks the end of Synanon, the model community, and the birth of Synanon, the self-serving fanatical religious sect."

Paul, who never intended to leave Synanon, ultimately settled in a small house in Berkeley with a platonic friend who had a couple of young children. One day, he drove into the driveway and, carrying the two bags of groceries he had taken from his car, was attacked from behind in broad daylight. A man wearing a stocking mask threw him to the ground and began beating him with a steel bar about sixteen inches long. While he was being beaten, one of the little boys he lived with stood watching and crying at the top of the driveway just outside a doorway into the house. Paul was lying on the ground on his back using his hands to try to shield his head, which received several blows from the pipe, several hard blows, as did the rest of his body. Neighbors began running to him. Some called the police, and the beating ended with the masked man walking to a nearby red car where a driver, also wearing a stocking mask, sat waiting for him. They drove away, and with so many witnesses the police were able to trace the altered license plate to Synanon, but could not prove it was the actual vehicle used since the original license plate had been restored by the time they found the car. But Paul, who knew every Synanon vehicle intimately, recognized the car when he was told about it. He even recognized it was an assigned car and knew the person to whom it had been assigned.

He went straight to the hospital, was patched up and decided to recuperate nearby at his brother's house. But the doctors had missed a hairline fracture in his skull around his sinuses, and early the next morning, Paul awoke having lost control of his hands and arms, which he observed flying wildly about his body. By the time his brother got him back to the hospital, Paul looked like a spastic drug addict. The doctors, who at first were convinced he was having some kind of reaction to drugs, were about to administer thorazine, but his brother vehemently protested, saying that Paul did not use drugs. One of the doctors decided to take a spinal tap and found that Paul had meningitis. Fluid from his sinuses had leaked through the fracture in his skull. The meningitis was advanced enough he quickly deteriorated into a coma where he remained for several days. With the help of massive doses of antibiotics he recovered almost fully, although the effects of the beating remain evident in somewhat slower speech and a slight limp.

In spite of the fact he recognized the car parked near his driveway on the day of his beating, Paul never believed Synanon was responsible. This is an example of the way we all compartmentalized our minds, manipulating factual details, using denial and perhaps even dissociation to see things the way we wanted to see them. I'm not certain this is a phenomenon exclusive to residents of cults, but it certainly was part of our communal make-up. He simply could not comprehend anyone who knew him could have done that to him and refused to entertain the possibility. Even in the face of the many stories of violence brought to him by former residents, in addition to his recognition of the car, he was unable to place blame with the community. Paul remained in a state of idealism about certain aspects of Synanon that could not be disturbed by mere facts, just like the rest of us. It was a technique we all learned well.

Finally, years after he was beaten, the district attorney called him and told him they knew who had ordered his beating and knew who had beaten him. The information had been revealed during a deposition. Almost a decade had passed. Paul was solidly based in the larger community as an accountant and builder, and by this time he gave information from the DA's office more weight than his need to maintain a certain innocence about Synanon. Paul sued and Synanon handed over money in settlement. Some would say Synanon used its insurance money to avoid a lengthy and costly trial, but I believe they paid him because they knew Synanon's culpability could be proved and they knew Paul would follow through.

SHARED RESPONSIBILITY

Synanon was structured so there was shared responsibility in all things. "Please let me first and always examine myself" was practically our mantra. If your roommate stole the dorm's laundry money, you were questioned as to what part you played in his or her misbehavior. "Why weren't you more aware of his activities? If your head wasn't stuck so far up your ass, you would have seen he was not acting right. You are here longer than he is, why weren't you more conscientious about watching the laundry money?"

131

An event that clearly illustrates this phenomenon was what we came to call "the Beam," the construction blunder that led to everyone, including all of the women for the first time, shaving their heads. A building on the Ranch property in Tomales Bay in the mid-seventies was to be renovated into a food service complex. The design included a kitchen in which all of the meals for the three Tomales Bay facilities would be prepared. The plan was for these meals to be delivered to the various dining rooms. The complex would also include offices, meeting and game rooms. An architect drew up the plans and there were several people heading up the construction crew. Engineer-types looked at the plans and made decisions about how they would be executed in physical terms, and construction foremen were responsible for the everyday details of the construction. There were also people who ordered materials, paid bills, and many others peripherally involved with the project. The point is there were several people who could have been held responsible for any piece of this project.

Midway through the renovation, as the story goes, Chuck took a walk through and had to duck under a beam that separated one part of the building from another. He asked when the beam was going to be removed and was told that it wasn't. The decision had been made to leave the beam intact, requiring just about every man and many women would have to duck when walking through the building. It was a crazy decision, but one made by someone, or some few people. It did not simply happen magically. Chuck began a rampage, "What asshole made this decision," and surely he was on the right track with that question. It really was one of the dumber blunders I can remember. Several people heading the project, all men, shaved their heads and hung their hair in plastic bags along the beam. This was a gesture to show they held themselves responsible.

Then, because everyone involved had to ask themselves how they could have avoided the mistake, one by one each person who worked on the project, down to the person who swept the floor at the end of the day, shaved his head to indicate that he, too, was part of the problem. *I thought it was a bad idea to leave the beam intact, but didn't game it because I don't have an engineering degree. I am not an architect. These professionals must know what they are doing. Who am I to challenge them? Buzz buzz off with my hair because I too contributed to this problem by not saying what I thought, by not being part of the solution.*

At this particular time, the issue of shaving heads to take responsibility spread when another incident, the sale of a camera by one of the women to another resident, came up for questioning. Because we were in a head-shaving mood, and because we were focusing on taking responsibility, Chuck patched into the game where the woman who sold the camera was being questioned and announced her head should be shaved. Let her take full responsibility for her decision—like the men do. The point being made was the camera should not have been sold, it should have been traded or given away. On the energy that comes of group participation, we took her off and shaved her head. Some of the women who had been involved in the beam project decided to shave their heads also. Why should only the men take responsibility? And before we knew it, everyone in Synanon was shorn for one reason or another.

Again, clearly there were a few people responsible for the decision to leave the beam intact. But there was little focus on them in particular. I don't even know why they made such a crazy decision. I do know they ultimately figured out another way to keep the building from falling down and at the same time allow people to cross from one side to another standing upright.

133

In the early eighties I was personally involved in an event that demonstrates this tradition of holding everybody accountable so that no individual or individuals are held accountable. Some of the children, who were then in their mid-teens, admitted that several years earlier they had smoked pot. The entire school staff decided to shave their heads, even those who had nothing to do with those particular children. One teacher refused. She insisted she worked hard, took good care of the children in her charge and was not about to suffer punishment and humiliation for something she had nothing to do with. We all shunned her.

Shaving my head along with most of the school staff seemed like a good idea. After all, we were our brother's keeper. That's what Synanon was all about. A funny thing happens to you when you participate in this kind of system. You feel a non-specific kind of guilt, remorse, even sometimes grief. But the problem is it is non-specific. There is no focus. There is no particular behavior you can address and try to correct in the future. You're never quite clear what the mistake or transgression was. Why did the kids smoke pot? Where did they get it? What does it say about them? What does it say about the kind of attention and supervision they were getting? What are the specifics of this situation that need to be addressed? Nothing specific is ever addressed. Generalized humility, shame and blame was the goal, with the participants feeling a fervent desire to do better, be better Synanon people.

When such an atmosphere of shared responsibility prevails, no one person can ever be held more responsible than anyone else. Each time a transgression occurred, large or small, we each looked toward ourselves to see what part we played, and it was primary for each of us to own up to our individual culpability. To this day many ex-Synanon residents are reluctant to place blame on key figures in the criminal activity of Synanon members. There was an organizational hierarchy. There were officers, people legally responsible for the affairs of Synanon. There have been few held accountable, although it is absolutely clear, in retrospect, there was a hierarchy of responsibility for the crimes committed.

THE GODFATHER AND CHUCK

When I heard that Paul had been beaten, I knew in a flash Synanon was involved. Who in the world would ever go after sweet Paul Runyon with such a vengeance as to almost kill him? Chuck had been bellowing in games about our enemies, which included all splittees—asking who was going to protect us from them? Today I know about first voice right voice, but back then if I even recognized first voice, I automatically dismissed it as wrong voice. Which is exactly what I did in the case of Paul. How the hell did I know any such thing? Did I see the beating? No. Could I testify in a court that someone from Synanon beat Paul? No. Grow up little girl. Put your imagination away. You don't *know* anything.

How had all of this come about? How had non-violent Synanon reached this point? I recently read an article in the *New Yorker* about the original *Godfather* movie, which we watched round the clock in Synanon for days in 1972. The article said the film… "was a perverse expression of a desirable and lost cultural tradition, filling people with longing for a family like that, a father who not only knew what was best but, if a guy was giving you a hard time, could have someone kill him." Did Chuck, probably in a game, say something like: *Who is going to do something about these people? Am I going to have to do everything around here? What do you people (referring to his staff, board, executive committee) get paid for? Do I have to do*

135

everything myself? I'm not going to be around forever, you know. When are some of you going to start taking care of the place? Are we just going to sit around and let these assholes walk all over us?

And then what? Someone from the game goes out and rounds up some guys with violent pasts—Viet Nam vets, armed robbers, guys with big rages and short fuses. Guys who were told when they came to Synanon that here they would talk dirty and live clean. And this person asks with fire in his voice if they would be willing to die or kill for Chuck. And they respond *yeah man* just as they are supposed to. And then with innuendo, just enough so they understand exactly what they are supposed to do, they are sent out with some money in their pockets and a nice car to teach this guy a lesson, and by way of teaching Paul a lesson, anyone else who thinks they know better than Chuck, who thinks he can disobey to the extent that Paul did.

I have no idea if it actually happened that way. I wasn't there. I didn't hear those words spoken directly and I couldn't testify in a court of law to such a chain of events, but....

DISOBEDIENCE AND INTEGRITY

Paul's story is important to me because it amplifies the relationship between Chuck's leadership and violence. It also clearly demonstrates the difference between disobedience and dissent. We had the game as a vehicle for dissent, but disobedience was forbidden. Disobedience happens when a person not only dissents from a decision or action, but clearly states that dissent, refuses to acquiesce to the mandate and makes public that position by challenging the author of the mandate. Many of us did not follow orders to the letter, did not do the exact amount of aerobics required, had a cigarette after we all quit smoking, or ate sugar with no stirrings of conscience. But no

136

one openly flaunted the breaking of these "small r rules." No one said, I have a cigarette from time to time and don't care what Chuck has to say about it. No one shared an anecdote about a visit to a parent during which they accepted a piece of their favorite dessert that contained sugar. In my circle, these indiscretions were executed in secrecy.

Paul opposed Chuck openly and went the extra step of trying to stop him from doing what he thought harmful. This brings up the notion of integrity. I always thought a person had integrity when he or she lived according to a code of behavior that was based upon right and wrong. I thought if a person followed the dictates of his conscience, paying attention to a code of ethics—that was action from integrity. But I have since learned such acts must also be made public. A person who believes in racial equality must challenge statements that cast aspersions on one race or another, not simply refrain from making such statements himself. It is in the challenging of things wrong that integrity comes into play. Just minding my own business and not harming others is not necessarily a life based upon integrity. One must make manifest what one believes is right to claim that virtue. It is difficult to do, and I'm afraid I fail at it more than I succeed. I am well trained in trying to ward off anger and go first for peace. But there are people angry at me still, so I have to ask myself why I don't act with integrity more often? If I am going to carry the burden of other people's anger, at least I can counter it with the warm glow of doing right.

Once upon a time I had the kind of integrity Paul has. There was a time when I included considerations of integrity in everyday decisions: asked myself what was the right thing to do in a given situation, right according to some hierarchy of values. When I first taught school in my early twenties, I was a true advocate for children and the fact that I was somewhat dull when it came to politics served me well in their pursuit. There was a child in my fourth-grade class named Denise. Shy and soft spoken, she had a difficult time reading and writing. One day as she stood tall in the front of the class reading with great concentration from a paper she had written, I sat in the back of the modern classroom straining to hear her soft voice, admiring her soft red hair, when I noticed a protrusion on the inside of her thin shin. Back then girls still wore dresses to school. The bump was not very noticeable, but at a certain angle it was clear something odd was in or on her leg. After school, I looked closely at it and asked her if she had ever noticed the lump. She said no.

I took her to the school nurse, who was concerned, and promised that she would contact the parents. Weeks went by and the parents did not return her repeated calls.

"Then go to her house," I said.

The parents did not take Denise to a doctor even after the school nurse spoke to them in their home. When I nudged her again, she told me she felt she had fulfilled her responsibility.

"I can't force parents to take their children to doctors," she told me.

I went to the principal, a congenial young man with a short blond crew cut who looked like he should be wearing sweats instead of a suit and tie.

"Mr. Johnson, Janet decided she has fulfilled her responsibility by telling Denise's parents she needs to see a doctor. They have not taken her, and it doesn't look like they are going to. We have to get her to a doctor."

"I certainly appreciate your enthusiasm and dedication Mrs. M., but we can only do so much. I will speak to Janet again and see if she has any additional ideas. You have done a wonderful job of trying to get this child cared for, but there is only so much we can do for our children. We are their teachers, after all, not their parents."

"Mr. Johnson, I see it as my responsibility to make certain Denise sees a doctor, and if you and the nurse are unable to accomplish this, I assure you I will."

"Mrs. M., it is really not within your sphere of responsibility to take any further action in this matter."

"Once again, Mr. Johnson, if you and Janet are unable to get her parents to take her to a doctor, I will."

The parents were finally persuaded by the nurse and the principal it was in both their and Denise's best interest to see a doctor. The result was that Denise had a non-malignant tumor deeply embedded in her shinbone. She had surgery, was hospitalized for a long time, and was out of school for a year during which she required extensive physical therapy.

I remember the kind of determination I felt. I remember not caring what anyone else thought—principal, nurse, even parents. My sense of what was right was so strong I took personal risks with little fear for my own future. I had no sense of politics or of protecting myself. It never crossed my mind that I had anything to lose by pursuing this line. My path was clear. I do not remember feeling particularly smug or even powerful when I accomplished what was needed for Denise. I changed schools that next year and didn't even follow up after I learned what was wrong with Denise. I simply felt I had done my job and the principal and nurse were not very good at theirs.

The Denise kind of thing happened more than a few times during the early years of my teaching.

I lost that in Synanon. My need to belong, to be considered valuable by those at the top, especially Chuck, became greatly magnified. It is not that everything else disappeared. It is not that everything I thought I valued disappeared, it is simply that they were reduced to intermittent thoughts while this need to belong took over.

I am materialistic and yet I owned almost nothing for twenty years. I am vain, and yet I was bald for ten years. I am a voracious reader, and yet I read very little in Synanon, and when I did read it was for escape and took the form of violent thrillers. I place great value on education and when I left Synanon with my thirteen-year-old daughter who is "intellectually gifted," she could not write a complete sentence that made any sense. (If I don't add that she graduated from UCLA magna cum laude, she will take offense.)

I lost my sense of self in Synanon, or another way of saying it is I gave up what I had come in with in exchange for what I perceived as acceptance. Paul reinvented himself in Synanon. His integrity, his values, all he was before he came to Synanon came clearly to the fore when challenged. When my core values were challenged, I rested on a lack of confidence. When I knew instinctively that Paul had been beaten by Synanon residents, I second-guessed myself, choosing to believe what those in authority told me.

MY PARTICIPATION

Everything in Synanon wasn't quite as dramatic as changing partners, vasectomies, or Paul's near-death beating. I have focused on these events to amplify certain underlying principles. Things this grand did seem to happen at strategic intervals, but between such events with a capital E, was the daily life of Synanon, that to the uninitiated might seem weird and bizarre, but to us was ho-hum. On a much smaller scale, what I call the darkness of Synanon took place in mundane ways, but ways that nevertheless contributed to a kind of lawlessness I see as having been systemic.

I collected money in the late seventies for what was called the CED Defense Fund. Everyone was encouraged to donate to this fund. We were told our enemies were after Chuck. All of the bad publicity about Synanon, all of the attacks upon Synanon by the press and various individuals, were because they wanted to cut the head off the organization. They wanted Chuck. And Chuck had to be protected at all costs. No matter what. He had saved our lives. He had created Synanon. We had all come to live in his house. How could we even think of allowing anything that would in any way jeopardize him? There was a constant barrage of emotional hype about the danger Chuck was in, and because of our proximity the rest of us were also vulnerable. We were on the lookout for a crazy ex-resident supposedly on a rampage in search of art works he left behind. There was a big uproar when one of our residents was supposedly shot at while driving a car. One now has to wonder why an even bigger fuss wasn't made. Why the police weren't called in. The resident who was shot at split immediately after, so he was never available to corroborate this information. One has to wonder how many of these scare tactics were manufactured or embellished beyond recognition.

Incident after incident served to lay the foundation for Chuck's army where lines were clearly drawn; the bad guys were anybody against Chuck. We were clearly the good guys, doing God's work and protecting the leader who made it possible for us to do so. With lines drawn so clearly the differences among us, differences of race, class, religion and individual struggle, were submerged and

141

relegated to places where they lay temporarily dormant. Each new "emergency" drew us into a more and more cohesive group.

The CED Defense Fund was established to supposedly set aside money that would be used for legal fees in the event Chuck needed legal representation. The fact that we had our own team of in-house lawyers didn't phase me one bit. The fact that we collected nowhere near the vast amounts of money that would eventually be spent on his various defenses never entered my mind. Facts just weren't that important. Details. I collected money, small amounts from people who had little to begin with and dutifully handed it up the line. From what I now understand, the money was used for the "outings" taken by Synanon men who beat people up and harassed others. It paid for nice hotels, good steak dinners, and generally to defer the costs of their involvement in the crimes for which they were commissioned. There was no paper trail.

I never had any idea of how the money was actually being used, and shortly before I left Synanon, I was in a game with a group of women who had decided to meet weekly to talk about things we had felt unable to talk about in regular games. Some of the women were married to men who disappeared in the middle of the night from time to time with baseball bats and guns and they talked about the various ways they had handled that situation. They had never discussed their conflicts about these events publicly until this series of games. Much of the information I heard during those games was new to me, and one time when I expressed surprise that one or another thing had happened, one of the women looked across the room, moved to the edge of her seat and said, "Why are you surprised, Alice? You were the one collecting money and financing these outings."

"What are you talking about? Money? Me? Financing the

outings? I don't know what you're talking about."

"Alice, you collected money for the Charles E. Dederich Defense Fund for months. What did you think that money was for?"

"I thought it was for Chuck's legal defense."

I was so clearly stunned by the accusation the women just burst out laughing at my naiveté.

I guess this is how institutionalized law breaking is done. Unwittingly, I was a part of the violence, but very far removed from it. I collected money that was used to accomplish violent ends, but I believed it was for something else. Only the craziest or weakest people actually went out and clearly broke the law, actually committed the violence, but there was a whole chain of people who were agents of violence most likely ordered by very few. The rest of us all knew just a little bit and usually it was some distortion of the truth.

VIOLENCE IN SYNANON: A KALEIDOSCOPE OF DETAILS

Starting before changing partners, and continuing for several years afterward, Chuck held forth at "Think Table" each morning in the Home Place lodge, and he had groups of people on "Home Place fellowships" who rotated through every week or so ensuring him a constant audience. The comparison was not lost on me when I read that Hitler held forth at lunch tables which were recorded as "Table Talk" in the journal of a young Bormann aide named Heinrich Heim. Chuck's monologues covered a wide range of topics—abortion, marriage, economics, politics—and featured Chuck's solutions to just about every problem therein. These sessions were taped. The plan was for his every word to be archived for posterity. During

143

these monologues the subject of Synanon's need for protection from outside enemies was often explored.

In 1977 and 1978 violence escalated. The Imperial Marines was the name given to a group of strong young men, trained for "combat," to protect Synanon. One-hundred-thousand dollars worth of guns and ammunition was purchased and stored in gun lockers on all properties. Alleged trespassers were violated in a variety of ways.

I had a desk in a large agricultural building called a Butler Barn. The interior was divided into sections, and I had my desk along with others next to what was called "The Connect," which was a hub like the front desk of a hotel. The Connect controlled the movement of the vehicle fleet, the telephone switchboard, housing moves—the everyday details of our comings and goings. All of a sudden two young men, outsiders, were brought in by the facility manager and some assistants who sat them in chairs not far from me. The men who brought them in were yelling at them.

"You think you are so tough trying to run two kids on bikes off the road with your pickup. Real tough guys. We're going to show you just how tough you are."

The two of them looked scared to me. They sat there for what seemed a long time while the men talked and met and finally decided to shave their heads as a warning and punishment for messing with our children. I watched them as they were held down into their chairs while two men shaved their heads, and I felt righteous. We were protecting ourselves.

I had never seen any of our children riding bicycles on the dangerous, windy road which was full of blind curves. If the children had been purposefully run off the road, we should have called the police. Maybe the pickup simply came too close to them around one of the many blind curves on that road and the kids got scared. Possibly it never happened at all, and the entire story was a fabrication to cover up for some impulsive act by someone trained to lunge at the slightest provocation.

I was once at the center of a complete lie in Synanon. A small group of us followed Chuck to Washington, DC in the late seventies. We bought an apartment building and many of the tenants remained in apartments while we took over other units as housing and offices. We installed a front desk in the lobby and handed out mail to the people who had lived in the building before we took over. Many of these people were not happy about this imposing group of about fifty with shorn heads and overalls taking over the lobby, putting in a front desk and holding our meetings in that public area. I was working on the desk one evening when a young man—small, dark, and quite official looking—came in for his mail. He was clearly not pleased at this new procedure, grabbed the mail out of my hand and turned away from my pleasant greeting. We had been asked to point out people who seemed hostile to us, and being the good girl I was, I told one of the men in the lobby that he had been rude.

Before I knew what was happening, two guys moved quickly toward the elevator where the man was waiting, grabbed him by the lapels of his suit and threatened him. Later that evening, in true *Godfather* style, the two men sat me down and told me that this was the story. When I handed the man his mail, he had said something obscene to me. I don't even remember what it was he was supposed to have said.

I am unable to tell a direct lie. I can do lots of other kinds of lying, but I can't say A if I absolutely know it was B. I don't think this is a moral thing, it just happens to be the way I am wired. I

145

never denied the *Godfather* version of the story, which was told over and over for a few days and then forgotten. I simply did not say anything when it was told. I never actually told either the correct or fabricated version of the story to anyone in Synanon. Years passed and I forgot the incident, but apparently the young man did not and he sued. I was living at the Home Place in Central California when an outside lawyer hired by Synanon called me in and asked me to tell him exactly what the man at the desk had said to me. Without a moment's hesitation, I told him the man had said nothing to me. The lawyer never asked me another question and thanked me for my time. We lost lots of money in that lawsuit. This is why I question every story ever told to us about violence and know at least in that one instance the story as told in Synanon was a complete lie. Just how many other men, fully-wired to act aggressively– protective in the event of any slight, lied to protect themselves can only be guessed.

There was constant conversation about how "they" were trying to get us. So much so the conversation became a blur, like background music. Every outsider was a potential enemy and paranoia ran rampant. The media were having a field day about Synanon, and committees within sprung up to harass media people who were reporting negative stories. I knew where the maps of some of the media moguls' houses were hidden and felt privileged to be "in the know." We were told the purpose of all this aggression was to make outsiders who challenged us realize we were a force not to be messed with.

The rattlesnake story was probably the most publicized story about violence in Synanon. A lawyer sued Synanon accusing the organization of kidnapping a young woman who came in for an interview in Santa Monica and within an hour of the interview, during which she said she wanted to think it over, was put on a bus and sent four hundred miles away to Tomales Bay and the newcomer program. Her lawyer, Paul Morantz, won the kidnapping case, and at Think Table Chuck bellowed for someone to bring him Morantz' ear in a jar.

Not long after, Morantz, returning home from work in Santa Monica, put his hand into his mailbox to retrieve his mail and was bitten by a rattlesnake. Along with the two young men who put the snake in the mailbox, Chuck was accused of the crime. The two men spent time in jail, Chuck pleaded no contest to conspiracy to commit murder and was put on probation and forbidden to run Synanon or play the game for two years, all the while proclaiming innocence and that his first amendment right of freedom of speech had been violated. I think he truly believed he could say anything he wanted at Think Table or in a game, such as, "Bring me Morantz' ear in a jar," and that was freedom of speech. As if words can't cause harm.

The official story was Chuck pleaded no contest because of his health. By this time we had been told Chuck had had a series of small strokes and his deteriorating health made it impossible for him to withstand a trial. This only added to our feeling of protection regarding him. As for what he said at Think Table, we were deeply committed to the idea that just as we could say anything we wanted in a game with no repercussion, Chuck could say anything he wanted at Think Table, which was an extension of the game. He was protected, just as we were supposed to be protected for saying what we believed in games. We were confused. By this time our world had grown very small and we did not bring more universal notions of right and wrong into our analyses of such monumental issues as

147

attempted murder and conspiracy to commit murder. We who stayed were satisfied to buy into the paranoia and the aggrandizement of unflinching commitment and loyalty which we were told was the only antidote to the danger that was very near.

Internally the conspiracy of silence was solidified during the two years Chuck was on probation for the rattlesnake case and forbidden to play the game or have anything to do with the running of Synanon. Everybody knew he was still both running Synanon and playing the game through his family and executive committee, at least everybody who lived at the Home Place or who spent any amount of time there did. We all listened to games at the Home Place and could hear Chuck yelling instructions in his wife, Sharon's, ear about what he wanted her to say when she "patched into" games from their apartment. In doing this we not only knew that he was playing the game, but he was letting us all know he was still there, very much in control. On rare occasions he even went into games, and when he did the cameras and recording equipment were immediately shut off.

Most of his executives lived at the Home Place and spent their time by his side at meals, sitting around the pool and in private meetings. They discussed everything with Chuck and knew exactly what he wanted them to do in all things pertaining to the running of Synanon. This was done with some discretion, but not much. One new resident, a young lawyer with an addiction problem, was outraged at this breach of probation, and when he split went to the authorities claiming Chuck was indeed still running Synanon and playing the game. Following this, I was asked to sign an affidavit stating Chuck was not playing the game or involved in the running of Synanon, and I signed it without even a twinge of conscience. There were many such affidavits swearing Chuck was fulfilling the terms of his probation, as well as others maligning the character and reliability of the person who made the challenge. His allegations were ultimately dismissed as unsubstantiated.

Starting in the mid-seventies and continuing until the end, Synanon was inundated with a stream of lawsuits regarding alleged acts of violence and harassment. In 1979 the IRS began an audit that lasted for several years. Both the justice department and IRS were closing in on Synanon.

Chuck made violent statements in many games and at Think Table, and almost every event Chuck participated in was taped and archived. We were told it was necessary to find references to violence in those tapes in case they were used against us in lawsuits. Large groups of residents listened to Think Table and game tapes and combed them for any violent conversation. I was one of many people enlisted to listen to tapes and my instructions were to log any violent passages I found. I was told we were logging violent references so that our lawyers could be forearmed in case of litigation. I had no idea these tapes had already been subpoenaed and the compromising passages we were all logging were being passed on to a group of people who then erased them.

THE MEASURE OF WRONG

All cults seem to move through a similar progression, and violence in response to paranoia is part of that progression. That Synanon became a violent organization is no big deal to me any longer; I now see that it simply followed a predictable pattern of such organizations. What remains a big deal to me, is that I lived in such close proximity to violence, and that I unwittingly played a part in its sustenance. As I read and hear more and more accounts of the violence in Synanon, especially from children who lived in the school, I learn more and more about my own struggle with integrity.

The sensors of my perfectly healthy conscience became dulled in Synanon—as when someone who is living just slightly beyond their economic means begins to slowly chip away at honesty. They mail bill payments without stamps. They take office supplies from work. They make personal long distance phone calls from their offices. They pad business expenses and use business credit cards for personal expenses, gas for their automobile here, a meal there. Pretty soon the lines of honesty–dishonesty have become blurred and they do not even know it. They have devoted too much energy to figuring out how to live on a level that takes just a bit more money than they have and all else falls into place under that umbrella. They, of course, do not see this. They are the core of the system they have created.

Often it is something very simple at the core of such a wayward journey. More often it is something simple along with something complex.

The simple thing that started me down this path was that from my very first encounters with Synanon, I was shocked and disturbed by the punitive nature of the discipline meted out to newcomers. The shaved heads for men, the stocking caps for women, the signs transgressors were made to wear around their necks declaring their crimes and misdemeanors, and the costumes sometimes worn were not disciplines that I was ever able to embrace. The randomness of punishments and the lack of distinction between serious and minor infractions were problematic for me. And this never changed. I always hated general meetings when newcomers sat on the floor and old-timers screamed and yelled demanding they admit to all of the things they had done wrong. The general meeting was a tool used for "tightening up" when things became loose, when disciplines broke down—when the signs of such looseness became obvious, or when major infractions were discovered—a theft, a lie, smoking, etc. I over-identified with the people sitting on the floor, and I under-identified with the people doing the yelling.

At first I told myself that I just didn't understand people whose lives had been so destructive. I didn't understand the workings of a mind that could allow an addiction to take over a life. I had to acquiesce my own negative reaction to that brand of discipline and let the people who knew about such things do their jobs. Gradually I just turned my back, compartmentalized that part of Synanon, put it in a box that I continued to react to, but looked at less and less as the years went by. I did this because, on the whole, Synanon appealed to me. It seemed to be a community to which I could belong, a community that offered me a kind of support and security that I needed so much that it overrode other considerations. I don't think there was anything terribly amiss in my early assessment. The problem arose when those negative feelings persisted in spite of my attempts at rationalizing them.

Not long after I moved in, this punitive way of modifying behavior spread into areas other than newcomer rehabilitation. All of a sudden my peers were being humiliated for what seemed to me to be honest mistakes. A miscalculation on a report by an accountant or bookkeeper was blown into an event of major proportion, and he was accused of lying, cheating, trying to do Synanon harm. He would be "busted" (lose his job), moved into less desirable housing, maybe even a dorm. These punishments never lasted very long, and people regained their jobs and housing, but the process was humiliating. I accepted this kind of treatment of my peers by telling myself that I really did not have all the facts, that the people making these decisions knew something I didn't, that they were better at such things than I was and all kinds of other bullshit that became so watered down in terms of believability that even I eventually had trouble convincing myself. But, still I did. I joined the majority in shunning the fallen person, often a friend, and participated fully in the "process" as it was laid out by those in charge. I was a very good friend Synanon style, but I am not proud of the way I conducted my friendships when things like this happened as they often did. It is one of the reasons why I cannot engage in discussions about what great friendships we forged in Synanon. I do not believe that this kind of treatment of people speaks of real friendship.

I did such a good job of convincing myself to accept something that was abhorrent to me that when this kind of punitive treatment crept into the school I stood by and even participated to some extent. Spanking logs were initiated and an entry might read something like this: *I had to knock Rachel down because she used a chicken towel to mop up some spilled paint.* This is an actual entry although the words may not be an exact quote. Had I been paying any attention at all—had I tried to find out exactly what that entry meant—I would have learned that Rachel, who was about five or six, was trying to help a school demonstrator (teacher) mop up some spilled paint and grabbed a chicken towel, which was part of a set of linens purchased especially for the school. The linens were red, white and black and were marked by chickens printed all over the fabric, thus chicken towels, chicken sheets, chicken pillowcases. They were a special purchase, but Rachel was simply trying to help and had no idea that chicken towels were different from any other. They were the only linens she knew, and I suppose her demonstrator thought she was teaching Rachel a lesson. Whatever the reasoning it was all wrong. The log entry was enough to tell an entire story about the school because, unfortunately, it was not an isolated entry. It was, in fact, one of the less compelling incidents in the lives of the children.

It is very easy for the erosion of principles to happen. First voice, that voice that comes from deep within must be trusted, but it is very easy to second guess that voice and to reject it, especially when you are young and somewhat adventurous. Principle and integrity, honesty, commitment and loyalty, terms that were thrown around Synanon like baseballs, are fragile and delicate, difficult to comprehend, and in need of great attention. By ignoring that first voice about something so important—the treatment of people—I set myself on a road that took me deeper and deeper into denial and an ostrich-like existence. I often wonder that I did not simply walk away at that early encounter. I think that had I known myself better, had I trusted myself more, and had I not had such a desperate need to find a place to belong, I would have decided that although I respected the work Synanon did, I did not think I could participate in that kind of behavior modification.

The other reason why I was able to accommodate so much that I should have rejected is more complex. I have always identified with the good guys, the innocent victims of mean-spiritedness. Who would want to identify otherwise? It never once crossed my mind as I pondered the holocaust, starting as a young child, that I could have been a Nazi or Nazi sympathizer or a kapo. It never crossed my mind that I would have looked the other way, or refused to help had I been a Christian German at that time. I believe in civil rights and placed myself firmly on the side of justice for all regardless of race, religion or economic standing.

I do not think this practice of over-identifying with "good" served me well. It has only been within the last ten years that I have recognized my own capacity for all that is base and inhuman, and I can now honestly say that I do not know how I would have reacted, or would react, in situations that call upon a higher good than the prevailing mode. I do know that in Synanon, I consistently chose to accept the prevailing norms even when I believed them to be wrong. For example, I always and unwaveringly believed that it was wrong to keep our young girls' hair the standard quarter-inch or half-inch short, but I kept it at that length, even clipping it myself for years and years. I had little courage to go against the majority opinion, the opinion of those in power.

As I look back over this part of Synanon, I find it impossible to just let it go—leave the bad and take the good. The popular response to such happenings is that "I didn't know anything," but I can no longer accept that. There was simply too much going on and there was too much publicity about what was going on both locally and in the national media. Granted, we were lied to more often than I care to admit, but in spite of that, we chose to not know what was going on. We chose, probably for differing reasons, to believe in Synanon's persecution and our right to fight it on our own terms.

If you believe it is wrong to commit or facilitate the commission of an act that causes premeditated harm to another person, it seems too simple a solution to let go of the fact that you lived in such close proximity by saying you didn't know. I have said that I didn't know what was going on, but as my memory came more and more into focus through the writing of this book, I remembered the two young men, held down against their will, getting their heads shaved and feeling righteous about it.

I do not have answers. I have questions that I need to address so that I can go forward with greater consciousness. Are these wrongs retroactive? The fact that I now recognize them as wrongs makes what I participated in no less problematic because I was unaware at the time.

"HOW MUCH GOOD WOULD A GOOD CHUCK DO IF A GOOD CHUCK COULD DO CHUCK?"

I am embarrassed I was so taken by a man who was in the final analysis mentally ill, corrupt and, what's worse, uneducated and poorly informed. He hardly read anything at all, did not have a formal education and believed his genius out-shadowed just about everybody else's intelligence. He grabbed a thought, idea, hypothesis from here and there and developed it Chuck-style to further his own and Synanon's ends. We went into little in depth because he got bored easily and quickly moved on to something new that stimulated him for a while. Something he could watch spread throughout Synanon like a wave pulling everyone along with him.

Even in Chuck's heyday, when his charisma captivated us and he was the acknowledged guru, founder, father figure and leader, I would have been somewhat embarrassed to admit his hold on me. We all had our ways of avoiding confrontation with ourselves about the fact we gave so much of our power to him. We were not stupid people, so we attributed greatness to a little man in order to shield ourselves from our own weakness. The story of Chuck is so much the story of *The Emperor's New Clothes* it gives new meaning to the fairy tale. It had never occurred to me such a fable could play itself out so graphically and I would be at the center of it. Now that we admit the truth about his gargantuan flaws, there are those who now claim Chuck had little influence over them.

One successful man who came to Synanon as a teenage square, says he got a business education in Synanon and Chuck's teachings had little effect on him. Others say it was the vision of living in community that attracted and held them, not Chuck himself. I have heard people say, "I hardly knew the man; he had little direct influence over me." Many ex-residents of Synanon take that approach to their relationship to Chuck, while others, like me, admit to his immense power over their every thought and action. Regardless of what people say, it seems unlikely anyone would have lived in Synanon for a long time as a distinctly separate entity from The Old Man, who was so at the helm and had so much power over the most intimate details of our lives. It seems as unlikely anyone from a loving, nurturing family would have chosen to live in such a community for any significant period of time.

There were as many traps in the path away from Synanon as there were on the path into Synanon, and I'm certain I have fallen into and stumbled around, as well as avoided, many. One of the traps I am aware of is to try to do Synanon better. Okay, we went astray, made some big mistakes, had our heads buried in the sand, were too tied to Chuck, but we've learned from our mistakes and now we can leave the bad and move forward with the good.

This last refrain, take the good and leave the bad, reverberates with compelling thoughts. Germany is full of people who lived through the holocaust and proclaim that yes, Hitler was evil, but he did build the autobahn. What a dismissive statement. Let's just move ahead and look at this remarkable road that serves as a model for the world and leave the rest behind. As if you can just break the good and the bad apart like that. I don't think so.

There seem to be a lot of people who believe you can separate the good and bad of Synanon that easily. I even heard one group put together a time line and everybody put blue dots on what they saw as the good things and red dots on the bad things. The dots formed a pattern: the early years were all blue, somewhere in the middle the red and blue combined, and the last years were all red. The group felt they had reached some consensus about the good and bad of Synanon by seeing this graphic time line and could go forward to build a better organization together armed with that consensus.

There are people out there who are still so tied into Chuck they are trying to do him and Synanon better: trying to set up better organizations than Synanon, trying to be genuinely altruistic, trying to lead without so much ego, trying to implement hierarchy that is not authoritarian, trying to build a community that is not a cult. Trying to take the good and leave the bad. I have to admit even Jerry and I, in setting up our business and family, were drawn into some of this kind of thinking at the beginning.

But good and bad are not so easily dichotomized. Synanon was a whole. It was a ball of clay with hundreds and hundreds of blue and red dots. It is simply not possible to pull them all apart in two neat piles in order to form a new ball of clay with only the good dots. It would take forever. It would never happen. It is distorted thinking. It is a way to never make changes and to keep things the same and not look at yourself too closely. It is a misunderstanding of how good and bad work, except in fairy tales and cults. Every action I am involved in contains both elements, which is why it is so difficult to lead a life of integrity and why so many of us fall short.

To all of you good people out there trying to do Chuck better, you can't. You can only do yourself better, and a better yourself is far better than the best Chuck you could possibly become.

PART IV
THE CHILDREN

THE CHILDREN

THE CHILDREN

Discovering Marin

Such silvery life courses through
that rainbow of oblivion
when I think of our hills in Marin,
The territory we owned and fostered
like a wild pet that our parents
were brave enough to let us keep.

We built secret forts with cold noses
and old tether ropes. We rode
unbridled ponies and balanced feathers
on our headbands. We blew milk
through our noses to make each other laugh
while secretly looking for our mothers,
whom we had lost along the path.

7/96 by Nicole Wisser

Synanon was an entity, a whole. It is a challenge to pull apart
the pieces to look at them independently. No matter where I go,
I find all of it tangled in a ball, and when I attempt to talk about
the school it is even more difficult because I have the tangle of my
own guilt and remorse to deal with. I cannot talk about all of the
children who were raised in Synanon; I don't even know all of the
children who are now young adults, some even into their forties. It
is important to remember just as all of the adults in Synanon were
quite different, so were the children. Some were born in Synanon,

160

some came with parents when they were older, after they had lived in nuclear families for five or ten years. Some of the children had a lot of contact with their parents, and some had little. Some were the children of squares, and some were the children of people who came for help and some had one of each for a parent. There were children who came to us after having been in foster care, and others who had lived with grandparents while their parent or parents were getting help.

The origins of the school were significant. Female newcomer residents, fighting to right lives that had turned to addiction, had a difficult time coping with the emotions regarding children left behind. Before the establishment of the school, many young women upon becoming sober couldn't deal with the pain of separation from their children and left before they were actually strong enough. The school made it possible for women to concentrate on repairing their lives with their children nearby, but not so close they were a distraction from their main order of business which was rehabilitation.

Today I hear stories about these young adults, and know many of them through my own girls as well as through friendships with their parents, and as far as I can tell they are a pretty regular bunch. Some have excelled educationally, some are amazing businessmen and women; one young woman has written and produced a one-woman show about her childhood in Synanon to rave reviews in New York and San Francisco; some have families of their own, some are having difficulty finding their niche, and a few have wandered out to the periphery of what is good for them.

As a mother I could have done worse. Through Synanon, I managed to find a way to shield my children from a part of my personality that was destructive and troubled: an anxiety and lack of patience that would have thrown me into the same rages my mother let loose against me. My relationship with my children was calm and loving, and we had good times together. I feel fine about that. What I feel bad about is what I did not do for them and what I generalize wasn't done for any of the children who grew up in Synanon: providing them with the constant, singular protective energy that is parenting at its best.

THE ACT AS IF

Just as shared accountability made it easy to fall down the rabbit hole where ends justified means, it is my belief the "act as if," the primary philosophy underlying behavior modification in Synanon, was a destructive force as it was generalized into the school and childrearing.

"Act as if" you are happy and you will become happy. "Act as if" you can lead a group and you will be able to lead. "Act as if" you can maintain a relationship and you will learn to do so. The "act as if" worked well in Synanon because so little attention was paid to individuals and individual differences. The newcomer was told to "act as if" he was happy and say a hearty hello to everyone he passed with a big smile on his face. If he "acted as if," soon he would really feel happy. If a relationship was difficult for you, "act as if" you loved the person you were with and before you knew it, you would love him. If you hated exercise, "act as if" you thought it was the greatest thing since sliced bread, and you would become comfortable with exercise. And so it went, each time a mandate drew resistance, reluctance, antagonism or fear, we were reminded the "act as if" was our most potent tool in terms of behavior change. You can be whatever you want, can live up to whatever standard is

162

set, overcome any obstacles by engaging in "the act as if."

The "act as if" is not a bad thing. We do it every day. Who among us wakes up to an alarm clock with glee? From inside the fog of sleep, we roll over, open our eyes against our will, think about something good that lies ahead—that cup of coffee and toast for me—and "act as if" we want to get out of bed. How many times a day do we suppress annoyance, and with a smile and as much patience as we can muster "act as if" we do not want to bite another person's head off? Without the "act as if" the world would be a mess, but it is not something that brings about meaningful change on anything but the most superficial level. It was possible to promote this philosophy in Synanon because change was supported both by peer pressure and the constant threat of punishment.

But I do not believe substantial change can be achieved by using the "act as if" as the primary mode of behavior modification. I do not believe change comes about without taking a close look at exactly what motivates us to behave as we do, understanding each of us has our own particular and peculiar internal energy system. Understanding alone cannot bring change, for if this were so, each insight would work to move us forward; unfortunately insights are a dime a dozen, and change is costly. The chief ingredient for change, as I see it, is will, and will cannot be imposed from without if it is to lead to substantive change.

I have made many changes over the past ten years. I wanted my relationship with my children to spring from a well of generosity rather than the muddled emotions of guilt and inadequacy I felt. I could "act as if" a little, but I had to do much more to find that well and tap it. I wanted to release myself from my mother, whose life I felt I had to make better. I over-identified with her aloneness and thought it was loneliness when it wasn't. My need to give to

163

her was a way of evaporating the reservoir of her anger that I still held in my middle. I have finally separated from her. I respect her aloneness, and I now give her only what she says she needs and wants. This did not come from acting as if. This came from reading and writing and revisiting feelings that were not pleasant and talking and adjusting the time and ways I visited with her. This change in our relationship has brought me great freedom and with it a new and constant affection for my mother.

Synanon was about change. We used to say the only constant in Synanon was change. The road to change sometimes brings anger, despair, grief, depression, confusion to the surface and the necessity to look to these emotions for meaning, for what they reveal about ourselves and our relationships. This was not acceptable in Synanon. Looking too deeply into things was derided as therapy. People who wanted to take more time with issues put together small, private games that became dubbed "back room games," and were frowned upon. Anyone who called someone their best friend was made fun of. The message was "do what we're doing," "one day at a time," "the game is not therapy."

Individual differences were not totally ignored in Synanon, but they definitely took a back seat to what was best for the group. The art of raising children requires there must be a group of people in a child's life who look at nothing else but that child's individuality and what is best for him and her alone.

THE SCHOOL

I am harsh in my criticism of the Synanon school, and many people who worked in the school or had children in the school are put off by the severity of my judgments. I have struggled with this because I feel only warmth for the children and many of the people who raised them, and yet I burst into flames whenever sentimentality about the school is expressed. I think this is because while I was comfortable at thirty looking at the whole, seeing the children in peer groups, thinking about them as little teams in training for running and implementing Synanon values, I now see them as individuals. When I remember them as children, I see little individuals whose uniqueness was subordinated and in many cases obliterated and I am angry that we did this.

In 1967, when I was twenty-four years old with three years of teaching under my belt, I saw the Synanon school as chaotic and spontaneous with a hodgepodge staff of street people, educated teachers, artists, but most of all people with a fire in their belly, a vision and dream to make a better place for children. And God knows we need better places for children.

The school drew me into it. The inspiration of conversion was Synanon's hook, and the school was its anchor. I moved into Synanon and began working full time as a teacher. In fact my relationship with the school was the most compelling relationship I had in Synanon. Some residents spent the majority of their time with the food services department, some in the newcomer programs, some on the sales team or in the business of sales support, some in data processing or accounting or the law office, but the majority of my time was spent with the school as my sub-focus. Synanon as a whole was my main focus. This was because I was a parent and a teacher. The raising and educating of children is the only area in which I had schooling, experience and some expertise. I worked in the school for about half of the time I lived in Synanon and had children both living in and visiting the school for the entire time of my residency.

We weren't afraid to throw assumptions in the air, and we weren't afraid to create new assumptions. The babies ate at low, round tables. Their food was placed right on the surface in front of them, and they ate with their hands. It was a riot. The food wound up everywhere, an adequate amount actually finding its way to the inside of their bellies.

Potty training was done in a big, bright toileting room after breakfast. Little potties were lined up and the toddlers sat, each with a book in their hand, while a "demonstrator" seated in front of the lineup told stories. Each time a child produced, he or she would bring the bowl from the potty to the demonstrator who made a giant fuss about taking it to a miniature-sized toilet for a flushing ceremony. We had no potty training trauma.

After potty training the kids were washed up, and they dressed themselves—sort of. This was actually a workshop and took as long as an hour. Help was offered when they needed it, but with great determination these toddlers did what they could for themselves and were given lots of time to do so. Each morning they made their little beds, which were low to the carpeted floor. They pulled crib blankets up over the mattress. Self-reliance. Independence. It was a good idea. But one I can see with hindsight was inadequate because it failed to incorporate other elements necessary to nurture young life.

With great enthusiasm and little intellectual temperance, we threw away far too many assumptions. We wanted children to spend the majority of their time with their peers; we wanted them to learn to depend, rely and learn to work with the children their same age. The flip side of this is adults, whether parents or demonstrators, who spent too much time with children were censured.

Adults were supposed to interact with children less rather than more. One lovely little baby boy, Matthew, spent a good deal of time crying when he was in one of the workshops with his peers. He was about sixteen-months old, and he would lie just inside the double doors that led to the hub where he knew adults were. He would stick his little fingers under the door and I am certain that was because he knew we'd see them even if we couldn't hear him crying, which we could. I would look through the glass at his little dripping face and actually remember saying, "I don't think Matthew was born to live in community." He clearly wasn't, but we knew it was best to not isolate him from his peers. We knew it was best to not give in to his demand for adult attention. If we just leave him alone, he will look to the other children for comfort. He didn't just then, but in time he, too, adjusted to the fact he wasn't going to get what he wanted from the adults.

The kids, even the very little ones, played together. They exhibited the best of family and the worst. When they played well, it was very well; and when they were mean they were very mean. Big time. Elyse and the two girls she was raised with are very mean to one another. Two of them are horrible, and the third takes much too much abuse without fighting back. I don't understand it very well, but I certainly don't like it. Julie, who is very close to her Synanon peer group, seems to have a tighter bond, although she experiences a lack of boundaries in dealing with her friends from Synanon. But they are deeply connected; and even when they do not get along, they feel the closeness of having a unique shared experience. There is really no way to describe Synanon to someone who did not experience it first hand. I have struggled with trying to do so for more than five years.

The children raised in Synanon, in general, do not have terribly good manners and, until they became much older, had poor speech and vocabulary. They used to sound like they were talking with

167

mashed potatoes in their mouths and tested uniformly low on vocabulary. To this day Elyse, who excels academically and is an avid reader, is still playing catch up in the area of vocabulary. I think this is directly attributable to the lack of adult–child interaction. They were isolated from the adult community, did not hear adults talking and did not engage in conversation that would elicit correction with enough frequency to make a difference. When Julie used to visit, the staff often commented on her good manners. She said please and thank you. This is the kind of thing a parent has to remind children of at least a million times a week to make it take hold, and we just didn't do that.

When I had been working in the school for a couple of years, it came to my attention some of the young preteen and teenage girls had begun menstruating and had not told any adult. I discovered one of the girls who actually had been raised by her mother for years before moving into Synanon, and had and still has a strong and loving relationship with her mom, had started her period almost a year before and had been using toilet paper in her panties to absorb the flow of blood. Their mothers were busy doing other things, leaving these kinds of responsibilities to the school staff.

I was horrified. I decided I could fix this problem, and to this day, young women in that peer group remember me as the demonstrator who made them watch those films about adolescence and sexual development, and taught them how to use tampons and sanitary pads, etc. They thought I was nuts at the time, but today tell me they appreciate the effort. But think about how arrogant and silly I was to think my undernourished effort could replace that mother–daughter intimacy that can only be built in small increments over many years. When the three girls I felt responsible for approached

168

puberty, I armed them with more information and supplies than they could ever need. Elyse was a very late developer, and by the time she began menstruating she was way over-prepared. But not so much so that we don't have private and lovely memories of working it out together. Unfortunately, I have subsequently learned it is not terribly unusual for girls to experience their first periods with little or no preparation.

In the early days of the school we read books about raising children that were popular at the time, books like *Summerhill* and *Children of the Dream*. We were determined to develop free children who were stimulated and challenged and taught both self-reliance and to trust their peers. Our motives were pure, and our enthusiasm for these ideals genuine, but we didn't realize trying to implement these philosophies in the midst of a therapeutic community was going to be problematic. The philosophy that guided the modification of peripheral behavior was harsh and punitive and relied heavily on humiliation and shame. Developing children who are free and self-reliant demanded the opposite. The philosophy of behavior modification far outdistanced the child-rearing philosophies we read in those books, and I believe, made it impossible to achieve those early goals.

MOTHERS

The people who worked in the school were called "demonstrators." Many of the demonstrators were wonderful women who from the moment they came on shift gave warmth and love to the children. They were innately generous and not particularly caught up in the politics of the day. Regardless of the constant changes in policy and structure and philosophy, they simply worked with the children, singing them to sleep, making up fairy tales about evil genies, hiking in the hills, nursing sick kids, making sure they got their snacks, lending a willing ear to disputes and drawn out stories from children who had not yet learned how to get to the point. These women worked long hours completing the details of their shifts long after they had officially ended.

The shifts in the school usually demanded demonstrators work on what was called "the cube." Each demonstrator had a counterpart. They worked either seven or ten days, ten hours a day, and then were off for seven or ten days. While one was off, her counterpart did the same job. This left children with one of two options. They could suffer loss when someone they were attached to went into "vacuum," which was what off time was called, or they could not attach in the first place. We, the staff, were considered interchangeable. A colder and more alienating name could not have been chosen for the people raising our children—"demonstrator." We believed if the children were raised by loving people who all believed in Synanon they would be fine. We considered their peers much more important to their development than any adults.

Following is a story I believe amplifies the absence of mothering in Synanon.

A thirteen-year-old child was having difficulty during the early 1980s. She was part of a peer group that seemed out of whack, negative, surly, disrespectful. They made fun of adults and talked amongst themselves about wanting to live elsewhere. Two of the children ran away. Chuck and Cicily said we should just let them go. They were negative and ungrateful and did not want to be here.

Let them go. One of the children had a parent on the executive committee, and a very aggressive mother who arranged a search party, and—armed with posters and several friends—began a search going from beach town to beach town down the coast of California. They actually found the girls and brought them home.

One child stayed in Synanon until "the end" and is doing well today as a young adult.

The other child, who I will call Jane, returned to Synanon after being found, and days into a process that was devised as their punishment, her father was killed in a motorcycle accident. His death was both sudden and unexpected. Cicily, Chuck's daughter, who was the executive committee member in charge of the school, decided Jane could spend one night with her mother, the day her father died. After that one night, she was to return to her "process." It is probably because so little attention was given to personal and private relationships no one protested the unfairness of this decision.

Cicily had absolute power over the school. She could decide entire groups should be punished and what that punishment should be. She could fire and hire people of her choosing to work in the school. She both hired and fired me.

Jane's mother acquiesced to Cicily's decision. When children "acted out," parents were invariably held responsible, most often by being blamed for not being able to "take positions" with their kids in support of the school. Their inability to be tough with their children was the reason the child was in trouble. So when a child was being punished, the parent was supposed to give full support, and in most cases stay away while she was going through whatever process was designed. When children excelled, it was invariably attributed to Synanon's magic.

A "process" means any variation on the theme of back to basics.

171

Possessions were taken away. Housing was reduced to bed and shelf, possibly in a tent or a newcomer women's dorm. Rigorous discipline was instituted. Early morning and evening runs. Work. Ten-minute meals in silence. No contact with anyone except the people responsible for ensuring that the process remained pure. Parents were off limits. These punishments were harsh, but usually lasted a comparatively short time, around a week or so, depending upon the age of the child.

Jane has had difficulty in becoming a healthy adult. I do not lay the blame for this on the way she was handled during this period of her life. I have watched too many children develop into adults who are surprisingly successful in light of their childhoods, and I have seen too many grow into disturbed adults in spite of childhoods that seem ideal. But I get very angry when I think of this tiny occurrence. It feels to me like drastic mishandling, total lack of empathy and the abandonment of all things nourishing. Where was womanhood in Synanon? Where was the feminine? To be sure, it was there lurking around the school, sneaking itself into the lives of children by some women who quietly gave warmth and love with great generosity. But it dove underground in the light of greater authority.

At the time, I did not think there was anything wrong with Cicily's order. I questioned whether or not it was a good idea to give Jane a night with her mother in light of the newness of the "process" and the seriousness of her offense. I supported "the father principle" demonstrated and espoused at every opportunity by Chuck. The father principle (conditional love) builds character. The father principle is real love. "Mother love" (unconditional love) is what makes sissies and dopefiends.

I think of these words today, and I shudder that they had any place in my life. Unconditional love is bad, it is what produces sissies and dopefiends. Unconditional love, the love that says you mean everything to me, that your wholeness is perfect and unique and I see it clearly, that without you the world and whole parts of myself would be irreparably diminished—that kind of love was dismissed with a sentence like "unconditional love is what makes sissies and dopefiends." I think I accepted it then because I feared I wasn't capable of unconditional love.

The content of what was said meant little. It was the context that meant everything. If Chuck said it, we came to attention. We did not disagree. We stayed within the lines he drew regardless of what we thought, if indeed we thought at all. If one of his executives said it, we listened because we were not sure if he or she were delivering Chuck's message.

Mother love survived in pockets and private places, but official policy was an extension of Chuck. Absolutely. The myth goes that Betty was the softer side of Chuck. I think that was true, but not in the sense of the myth. She did not stand alone strong and equal, eye-to-eye. She was an extension of her husband and when her softness suited him, he used it. When it did not, she tucked it in and could deal verbal blows and make punitive decisions with the best of them. Synanon was a male culture in spite of the fact we trained women to be auto mechanics, saluting ourselves at every opportunity at our enlightened feminism. In the same way we announced the mere existence of the school liberated women, so we had nothing to complain about.

It is in the little stories of people's daily lives—stories small in light of changing the world, but monumental in the lives of individuals—that the death of the female principle can be most clearly seen. Children suffered disappointments regularly because their individual needs were deemed of little importance and there were pathetically few people around to make things better for them. When we complained or took up the cause of an individual child, we were told—more than I care to remember—the child was just fine; it was us, the adults, who were having the problem.

SARAH

Sarah had been a good kid. Her mother, Jan, was one of my best friends. Sarah is about the same age as Julie. I loved Sarah, and she was my kid Synanon-style. I kept a constant eye on her, and we did special things together. When Sarah was six her dad, who was in his sixties, died of cancer. He had been ill for a long time. On the day of his death her mother was involved in adult ceremonies that were being held for him, and I invited Sarah to come and spend the night with me. This was not unusual. Jan felt just fine about it. She knew Sarah was in good hands with someone who loved her, and she had her community responsibilities. This was not odd. It was the Synanon way. Once someone said in a magazine article we were all interchangeable.

Sarah was, and still is, slight and blond and very pretty with chiseled model-like features; she grew into her teenage years with a strong sense of isolation. She hated her shorn head and everything else about her life that made her different from kids her age who did not live in Synanon. She was deeply ashamed of everything she was told she was supposed to be proud of, and the only feedback she got about this was to be humiliated and punished for her lack of gratitude.

She is riding through the nearest town on a school bus with Synanon plastered all over the side. Looking out of the window she spots a boy she knows, someone she met when she was going to public school. Just as his eye is about to catch hers, she ducks, murmuring as only a self-conscious newly-teenaged girl can, "God, I hope he didn't see me. Did he see me? Oh please God, I hope not." When they returned to the Strip, word about Sarah's behavior on the bus spread, and a meeting was set up where she was stood in front of the entire school and told she was an ungrateful brat who should be proud of Synanon, proud of our differences, proud of wearing her hair short, blah blah blah.

We weren't always being hammered on. Things would relax. Hair would creep to a half-inch instead of a quarter-inch. Overalls would be worn less than every work day. That cramp in my hamstrings still hurts, I think I'll pass on aerobics today. And some people never paid much attention at all to the myriad small rules. Remember, there were a lot of disordered people in Synanon whose consciences didn't function on all cylinders. In addition to secret smokers, I've been told a whole group of men would take kids to town, to a big fifties-like ice cream parlor and buy them "sugarless sundaes." Oh, and yes they too had "sugarless sundaes," with the kids.

Sarah's hair has grown. It is blond and wispy. Her grandmother is visiting and suggests she give Sarah a perm. Jan nods her consent and they pile into the pickup truck outside the small house they live in, up the road a bit from the main Strip facility, and drive to a nearby country general store where, sure enough, there is a home permanent kit on the shelf. Sarah can hardly believe her mother said yes. She loves her life this afternoon, all the attention, her mother and grandmother fussing over her hair, talking to her and over her head to each other, her grandmother explaining each step of the process. Sarah is in heaven, and the results are even more than she expected. She feels like a member of the human race, at least the kid human race. She can compete. She looks beautiful and she looks like other kids, kids in the real world, in real families. She does not look like every other girl in Synanon. She is enchanted with herself. For a few brief minutes.

Later that same afternoon, the phone rings. They are told a general meeting is being set up for the kids—now. General meetings are bad. Everyone is pulled together, sat on the floor and yelled at for some infraction. Someone did something and we will all have to sit until someone "cops out" or someone else "cops out" on the guilty person. Sarah is well acquainted with general meetings, but she is still too excited about her hair. She piles into the same pickup truck with her mom and grandmother that she rode in a few hours earlier. She is miffed, but her emotions are still blurred by the euphoria of finding herself both acceptable and beautiful—a feeling that every woman remembers about girlhood because it comes as a flash of lightning in a sea of doubt.

Cicily addresses the group. *Is anyone watching the store here? Has anyone taken a look at these kids lately? Has anyone noticed they all look like any other kids? Has anyone noticed their dorms are a mess, there is no crispness, no teeth and fuzz? These kids have all forgotten their drills. They've forgotten who they are. Who we are. They've forgotten that Synanon is different. That Synanon is better. You kids are better kids than other kids, and it's because you live in this community. It's because my dad built you a school and a community within the community so you could grow up free without the restrictions that come with living in an adult world. It's back to basics. I'm going to get some fresh blood in the school, some of the kids who grew up here will be taking care of you. You are going to begin marching, you are going to begin wearing uniforms to school once again and you are all going to get your hair cut. Hasn't anyone looked at them recently? These kids have long hair for Christ's sake. Get the clippers.*

Just as Sarah realizes what's happening and stiffens her body for flight, her mother signals her stepfather to go and restrain her. Chairs have been pulled into a line, clippers have materialized and children are quietly moving in and out of the chairs submitting unhappily, once again, to what they know is inevitable.

Sarah begins struggling against her stepfather and another parent steps in to help subdue her. Her body is like steel wires poking out in all directions and they are trying to round her arms and legs so that she can be seated and clipped. "Let me go," she screams in what is naturally a throaty voice. "Stay away from me! Don't touch me! Let go!" It takes the strength of two men to move her tiny body across the floor. She becomes hysterical. In the confusion her grandmother is forgotten. As she is being dragged across the floor, she turns her head to see someone escorting her grandmother away from the scene, but not before she catches the look of confusion in the older woman's eyes.

The two men finally get her over to the clipper station and a third person begins clipping her hair. Already hysterical, she finds new energy in this outrage. Screaming, crying and flailing her arms madly, an elbow or an arm or a hand makes contact with her nose and blood begins flowing from it. Blood and snot mixes with tufts of hair shooting wildly around her as the clippers grope and prod for the soft yellow curls.

She lost her hair and her perm, but her resolve to never be subdued was cast in stone.

A PROCESS FOR SARAH

Synanon was like a big pot of water. I moved in when it was lukewarm and every so often the heat was turned up so slightly I hardly noticed. I got used to it. By the time Sarah was a teenager I was so thoroughly compromised that all of my information about her came from her mother, who had no access to her. Jan got her information from Cicily, who had little access to her. The young adults, taking care of what by now had become an entire peer group of nasty, hostile teenagers led by the most hostile of all—Sarah—reported to Cicily. Now, one of the things that puzzles Sarah more than anything else is that no one ever sat her down and said, "Hey, what's going on?" And then listened.

I had this other relationship with Cicily, one I initiated and had mostly to do with the school. Every so often a policy involving the children would gnaw at me so much I would feel a pressure I just had to release. Like the length of the kids' hair. What happened was, at lunch tables Cicily hosted she invited her guests to bring up issues they wanted to discuss with her.

"Cicily, I know how you feel about the kids' hair, but I really think they need a chance to experiment with their appearance, which in reality is experimenting with their identity. They need to have long hair, short hair—and they especially need to be recognized as girls. Even though we pierced the kids' ears, they are constantly referred to as boys. And they hate that, as they should." I introduced this conversation on at least two occasions.

I was never surprised by her response. *I can't believe people mistake them for boys. But even so I am not going to give in to everyone's desire for Synanon to become like everyone else. This is all you're saying.*

Everyone wants us to stop doing something. Why can't we eat sugar? Why can't we grow our hair? Why do we still have mandatory aerobics? Why do we have to wear overalls to work? Some of the sales people actually think we need to let our hair grow because we're losing sales because of bald heads. Really! Doing things as a group is what makes us powerful, makes it possible for us to do the work of Synanon. It's great they have short hair. They look great."

In this way, I contrived an innocence. At least I said my piece. I relieved the pressure of repressing what I knew to be right, but I did not effect any change at all by doing so. I got my lecture, which was better than feeling the pressure that built up from having done nothing at all. I should have let Elyse's hair grow, insisted it not be clipped, but anything could have happened to me, including being asked to leave. I just didn't have it in me to go that far.

Sarah and her entire peer group became surly and hostile. This peer group consisted of six or seven young girls, and I cannot state too strongly it was very different for the boys, who were distinctly different and were looked upon differently. They seemed to me to be more diverse in their attitudes and less overtly hostile to adults. I do not feel equipped to analyze them as a group, other than to repeat they were distinctly different from the girls in attitude and to guess they stood a better chance of survival being males in an extreme authoritarian patriarchy. That Sarah's entire peer group was acting out their anger and hostility might have been a signal something was wrong with their lives, but that is not how the children were ever looked upon. They were looked upon in much the same way dopefiend newcomers were. There is a problem in that group. They are negative. Let's fix them with hammers. Never were they rubbed with velvet cloths until we could see their shine.

Sarah and the rest of her peer group, who were all thirteen and fourteen, were put into a process. They were moved into tents, stripped of possessions, made to run in the morning and evening, and worked all day painting the outside of buildings in bright colors. It was a grueling process, but Sarah had made a clear decision she was not going to break, which would have meant apologizing and adopting a proper Synanon attitude of teeth and fuzz.

It is a warm summer evening and the girls are being led on their before-dinner run. Sarah is tired. Beat. She is starving and dirty and wants to shower and eat and retire with the girls for their nightly session of making fun of everybody and laughing themselves to sleep. She is taunting the leader and the girls are all following her. Every time the young woman at the front of the line turns forward, they make clown-like motions and slow down. When she goes to the end of the line, they really slow down. She changes the order of the line. She yells. She has clearly lost control of this group. A man runs by the girls and, assessing the situation, joins the leader to give her support. Sarah does little adjusting of her attitude. "What are they going to do to me? What's left to take away?"

When they reach the turnaround point in the run, at the end of the Strip approaching the dam and a field of trees, the man tells Sarah to stay behind while the others run ahead. He orders her to run correctly. She refuses. He pushes her. She moves away from him. He follows and continues to push because she is not running fast, straight and earnestly enough to indicate to him she takes him seriously. Sarah does not take anything seriously by this time, except getting out of Synanon.

Her temper flares. Who is this man? Just because he has a kid he thinks he can just step in and order me around. She starts walking.

He pushes her. She screams at him, "Get your fucking hands off me." He pushes her and she falls and she is kicking him and he grabs her tee shirt and is dragging her along the asphalt runway. By now they are passing office buildings. Sarah is screaming, "Child abuse," which is one of the things runaways have told authorities to keep from being returned. The kids know this is a potent accusation. They are heard. Someone comes out to put an end to this encounter and the next day Jan is told Sarah can no longer stay in Synanon. She is sent to live with her grandmother.

Nobody was paying attention. The young women entrusted with seeing the process through were first of all trying to figure out what would please Cicily, mostly by reading between the lines. *You know what I mean…the way you were positioned when you were teenagers… you're so much closer to their age…you can identify with them…they can identify with you…they'll come around…they're really good kids, but they need a good swift kick in the ass…back to basics…take away their possessions and privileges…you know what I mean…you know what to do.*

The young adults heading up the process were also passing on the legacy. They had to go through this. They remembered one of their peers, a slow runner, being kicked in the behind because she lagged behind on the daily five-mile runs they had to make only a few years before. She was kicked over and over, fell sometimes, got back up, ran, was kicked again. *Now it's your turn. You'll grow behind it. We did.*

Jan was playing her role by staying out of the way and letting the process work, being a good Synanon parent. She could use her game to talk about her feelings, but out of the game a stiff upper lip and total support for the process was required.

181

The man on the run was playing his role. This is a gentle man, by nature. Honest. He was taking responsibility in a system that spelled responsibility with a v, or an f. V for violence. F for force.

I talked to Jan about Sarah who talked to Cicily about Sarah who talked to the young women in charge of the girls who told her what they thought she wanted to hear. Nobody talked to Sarah. She was a kid. Kids occupied the lowest rung in the class structure.

MY DAUGHTER ELYSE

Although Sarah was not one of my biological children, she was one of the children in Synanon I considered mine. I felt great affection for her, and still do. Yet, when I look at this story, which is essentially her memory of this experience, my role as a responsible parent in an extended family cannot be taken seriously. I cannot speak for all of the other parents in Synanon, and I concede some did better than I, but, in general we all acquiesced to decisions about our children that were simply not based on love.

When Elyse was about six, Cicily decided we no longer needed a school. The kids were old enough to be taken care of by the community at large. Staff was severely reduced and the attention given to the kids was seriously diminished. I might also add here that when Cicily's daughter, who is older than Elyse and younger than Julie, was a young child in the school, Cicily saw to it her peer group got the best housing and best staff. Her own daughter was given private piano lessons and valuable gifts from her grandfather, which the staff had to keep track of. It is not as if these things went unnoticed, but no one ever had the temerity to ask why her daughter should be given privileges and opportunities not available to ours. Never.

Vannie's mother, Mary, Tamara's stepmother, Rosie, and I took up the slack and supervised the girls on a daily basis. We spent a great deal of time with them, more time than just about any parent had been allowed before us. It was not a burden, even though it was not always easy to arrange coverage because of our schedules. We had a good time with each other and with the children. This little group became my family in Synanon.

When we left, Elyse was thirteen, and as a new member of the larger community she began observing families. She was attracted to children in school whose parents were strict, and she measured my parenting by their rules. She clearly equated love with boundaries, and if I missed a cue, she reminded me.

"I came in after curfew last night. Did you notice?" Yes, I did notice. She was about five minutes late and I had let it go.

Shortly after we left Synanon, Elyse tried to talk to me about the way she was raised. She had feelings of abandonment, felt Max and I had not been present enough in her early years, and resented the fact other adults had disciplined her. She has a strong sense this is wrong. Only parents have the right to discipline their children. I was singularly dismissive of her complaints, reminding her about how good she had it in Synanon compared to the children who came before her. Think about how little exposure they had to their parents. I told her, and meant it—she had been practically indulged. By the time I was able to embrace and admit the fact—her feelings were indeed valid: I had been just about as absent from her early years as I had been from Julie's—she had forgotten most of the specifics of her childhood and was left with a dull resentment and active anger toward me. I am fortunate that my children want a relationship with me badly enough to work with their hurt and anger so we can continue to develop our love for one another.

Elyse did remember one incident that she shared with me. One Sunday afternoon when she was about ten years old, she came up to the housing that I shared with Jerry to hang out. She and Jerry were lying on the floor, their heads propped on cushions from the couch watching a football game when she fell asleep. I carried her to my bed and she slept soundly all afternoon. When she woke it was time for her to return to the school. She was distressed but tried not to show it. She asked if we could have dinner together later that evening. I told her I had plans. She was devastated and walked down the hill to the school feeling she had blown the entire day with me and had no idea when a like opportunity would present itself. Time like this—long hours spent alone with me—did not come as often as she would have liked, and she had wasted the entire afternoon sleeping. I was oblivious to her disappointment and told her I'd meet her for breakfast the following morning. She did not show her feelings because she had so often been overpowered by adult indifference.

Earlier, when Elyse was six, Synanon left Marin County and moved to Central California. I moved before she did, probably a couple of months earlier. The school was the last to leave. One day, while we were separated, she fell off her bike and hurt her arm. Elyse is not a crier, although she was a child who sought adult attention more than was considered acceptable. After the fall, she sat down on the steps of one of the buildings, kind of whimpering, and when one demonstrator passed her on the way to a meeting Elyse said her arm hurt. The demonstrator looked at her arm, and perhaps acting off of Elyse's reputation as an attention seeker, told her to go and play, there was nothing wrong with her. That same demonstrator came out of the building a while later. Elyse was still sitting on the steps complaining about her arm, and the demonstrator insisted she leave the steps to go and play. Several minutes later, Beth came to the steps of the building and, seeing Elyse in distress, stopped to see what was wrong. Whatever Beth was about to do was put aside, and she got Elyse to a nurse who subsequently took her into town to the hospital for an X-ray, staying with her until her broken arm was set and put into a cast. After she returned, Beth called me to let me know that she was fine, the break wasn't serious and all was well.

I could have acted as either of those women did depending upon my mood, the time, who the child was, what I was about to do.

These were not major incidents of dramatic proportion, but I think these kinds of little disappointments happened often enough to put big cracks in the foundation of our children's trust in primary relationships.

CRIMES AND PUNISHMENTS

I cannot pinpoint exactly when the treatment of children in the school began mimicking the treatment of adults in the newcomer program. When the school was established, most of the children belonged to adult newcomers and most of the people who worked in the school were the parents of these children. In 1970, when I moved into Synanon along with many other squares, the complexion of the school began to change. Its ranks filled with the children of squares, the staff began to include square women like myself, and many of us were professionally trained.

I lost custody of Julie because the judge felt I had abdicated my responsibility to her by placing her care in the hands of people barely removed from their lives of crime and addiction, people of questionable demonstrated character. I now agree he was essentially correct. Shortly after I lost custody of her, the hiring policy of the school changed, and no one in Synanon under a year was allowed to work in the school. If an addict was hired in the school after he or she had been in Synanon for a year, he had to be closely supervised and trained for a long period of time.

It was in 1972 that Chuck promoted the use of corporeal punishment in what was called "the punk squad," which was the name given to a program for juvenile delinquents sent to Synanon for help. The analogy he used was that of a mama bear who knocks down her cubs and then hugs them. The idea was to knock them down, swiftly, to get their attention. This was contrasted with the prolonged torture of being lectured or punished. Just knock them down when they do something wrong. This system of dealing with undesirable behavior found its way into the school, and the spanking logs in the lower and middle schools was how the school dealt with possible abuses. The behaviors that were subject to corporeal punishment—the ping-pong paddle for younger children, the fist for teenagers—ranged from micro-misdemeanors to normal child testing of boundaries and minor acting out. It is my opinion corporeal punishment had no place in the school because our kids were basically good, and generally well behaved.

Property destruction was an oft-repeated issue and included all infractions major and minor having to do with the way our communally-owned materials were mishandled by the residents, including children. The other side of property destruction was proprietorship and all object lessons concerning property were supposed to lead to a greater sense of proprietorship. But proprietorship was not the same as ownership.

We were sanctioned against borrowing; neither a lender nor borrower be, and I have carried from that admonition the understanding that if ever I loan something, I must allow for the possibility it will not be returned. Most things were communally-owned. Furniture, bedding, housing and automobiles were shared and passed around from custodian to custodian. We were responsible for the maintenance of all we used, but we did not get to own any of the items. Some things were passed to us in good condition, some were fair and others were used more than we might have been happy about. We were expected to act with proprietary interest regarding all things belonging to Synanon.

Infractions were as colorful as the people who resided in Synanon. Anything thrown away was considered property destruction. A paperback book had been found in a dumpster and the director stood before the entire Strip population before games one evening bellowing, "Who threw this perfectly good book away? I want to know what person is so careless with Synanon property that they would throw away a book." When no one from the gathering responded he concluded with, "Find out in games who did this. I want to know."

I happened to be in the game with the teenager who admitted throwing the book away. "Why did you throw it away," I asked the feisty young girl.

"Because it was missing about forty pages."

"Why didn't you say so when Alan asked who had thrown it away?" I innocently posed.

"Are you crazy? All I needed was for him to decide I wasn't telling the truth or for him to have made an object lesson of me for everybody else who might have thrown something away. No thank you."

There was a small chicken coop near the entrance to the Ranch property in Tomales Bay that someone maintained more as a hobby than anything else. One evening, at twilight, just after they finished dinner, two ten-year-old boys wandered into the coop. One of them picked up an egg and spontaneously tossed it to the other boy who caught it easily. *Let's try this a bit further away from each other. How far away can we get and still catch the egg with ease?* That experiment was easy, breaking only one egg as they found the proper distance for egg tossing. With itchy fingers they plotted to find out how hard they could toss an egg and still catch it whole. Several throws later, experimenting with both distance and force, they discovered the smashing of the eggs was about as much fun as the tests that had started the whole affair. Many eggs and a whole lot of mess later, they lost interest and with absolutely no thought to what they were leaving behind, or even that they had done anything wrong, continued on to their evening activity.

An easy confession was extracted after the atrocity had been discovered. The boys were Synanon pros and were less careful than the girls in trying to avoid landmines, taking their punishment with resignation. It seemed fair. They could accept they had destroyed property and would take their medicine, which was to wash motorcycles (proprietorship) on Saturday. The rest of their peer group was included in the punishment. Where had they been? Why hadn't they known what the two drifters were up to? And anyway, if these two boys were so blatantly unaware of the importance of taking care of property, it follows their entire peer group could stand a lesson about proprietorship.

We took this very seriously. No one dared to wink behind their backs and express that they must have had a ball breaking those eggs. No one rejoiced that a couple of kids had broken away from the pack and found some harmless mischief. Property destruction was a very serious offense. And any chance to straighten out a child was taken.

The children owned no property at all. They moved constantly from bed to bed, from dorm to dorm. For many years clothing was communal, with children owning only their shoes and winter jackets. We never could understand why they never seemed able to remember where they'd left their jackets at the end of the day. Underwear, pants, tee shirts were pulled from shelves in each dorm at the start of the day. In later years, children were outfitted in their own clothing with their initials indelibly printed on pockets, tags and waistbands. A child could have a pair of pants with as many as five sets of initials on them. Toys were communal, gifts were not encouraged.

When Elyse was about ten, and she and Vannie and Tamara each had their own modest wardrobes, someone who had dropped in to spend some time with them, discovered they all borrowed each other's clothing, an activity that expanded their respective wardrobes by quite a bit. What were we teaching our children, the woman with fresh eyes questioned. Didn't they know to neither a lender nor borrower be? Who was watching the store and making sure the children learned solid Synanon values? The girls were forbidden to borrow from one another. They were unable to comprehend this admonition, having shared every single thing material including the air they breathed since they were born, and we as their parents were supposed to support this completely invasive order. I turned the other way mostly because I had more pressing issues I was dealing with, like trying to get the clothing they did have assigned to them washed properly so they were not walking around with a design of stains on just about every item they wore. How did anyone think we could begin to instill private ownership in three little girls who had shared everything for their entire lives? It probably would have been a good idea, had it not been so random and out of context. And since, by this time no one took the school seriously, this new edict simply fell through the cracks.

I now wonder how we ever had the nerve to punish children for property destruction or borrowing without first instilling the concept of ownership and the pride that goes along with that.

The way we handled such things as the care of property and individual ownership vs. communal sharing was done poorly, in a slipshod and random manner, with enough hypocrisy to sink the community. Waste and excess was common among executives. Shooting from the hip and not following through was routine with the kids. We looked at a symptom as if it was the disease, and even when we tried to follow a symptom to its root cause, we almost always chose the path that would lead us where we wanted to go, not where truth resided.

PHILLIP

I am about to celebrate my ten-year anniversary of being out of Synanon. I am conflicted about the way I parented my children, although I am not conflicted about the way I presently parent them. I no longer have difficulty knowing no matter what, those relationships are my priority. I am also conflicted about the responsibility I had for other people's children in Synanon. I have met enough "normal" people in "normal" families to know mine is worse than some and better than a lot. I have watched at close range enough parents parent their children with creativity and dignity to know I fell short, and I have met enough children of such parents to see that while some of them turned out lovely, others fell far short of expectation. Basically it's a crap shoot, but I wish I could say I did my best, and that my best was good enough. My best was not good enough then, and now, although still imperfect it is quite good enough. Jerry jokes that between the two of us we make one very good parent.

Recently, Julie called me in distress. Had I heard about Phillip? Someone told her he was in a coma in Eureka, California. Phillip was born six weeks after Julie, and his mother, Beth, and I exchanged babysitting when they were little (Beth is also the woman who took Elyse to the nurse who finally had her arm set). We all moved into Synanon at about the same time, and Julie and Phillip remained friends throughout their lives. Beth and I remain in touch, but were not intimate. We live on different coasts. I had met Phillip on several occasions after he returned from years abroad where he experienced adventures both dangerous and courageous. He was a young man who cast a big light, kind with impeccable manners. He was brilliant, funny and as handsome as they come. Six-feet-and-three-inches of lean body topped with a smile that, his father said at his funeral, revealed acres of white teeth.

I found out Phillip was indeed in a coma. After a hang gliding accident off a mountain he landed in an empty field and struck his truck, which was the only thing in the vast field. He suffered massive head injuries. He hung on for a couple of months fighting to surface from some depth none of us understood, and his mother generously allowed a few of us to visit and be present during this difficult process. It was my first conscious experience with serious illness and

191

death, and it was a privilege. It was a privilege to watch Beth and her husband give more than I thought people were capable of giving. It was a privilege to watch Phillip fight and struggle and for me to offer any comfort I was able to give. It was a privilege to watch doctors and nurses of infinite kindness and to listen to his father and stepmother share their hopes and fears. The response to Phillip was awesome. Letters, faxes, presents, artifacts, healing devices arrived by the dozens. The messages that came to him overflowed with love and concern, and I read story after story about him as a child and young man—absolutely hilarious stories and stories that spoke of his determination and courage.

My emotions were clear. They did not have much to do with Synanon, they had to do with my identification with Beth, my history with both her and Phillip, my concern over Julie's distress and with the fact that I had created a space within myself for community. I no longer needed to find a community. I could make community. I could bring a small parcel of community where it was needed. It was personal. It wasn't communal, but it contained community.

His friends were drawn to him. They visited regularly, flying in from all over. He was moved to Laguna Beach to a room with a panoramic view of the ocean. He died. His brain was no longer regulating vital body functions and he suffered horrendous sweats and muscle spasms. He was in distress. He died early in the morning when no one was around. The nurses told us that is often the way it happens. It is easier to let go when no one is around.

His funeral was held in the home of a good friend of mine. Some women—women from long ago, women I'd met before I moved into Synanon, and presently had limited or no contact with—joined me in setting up the physical space for the funeral. We worked together like a well-oiled machine. Egos were put aside. Leadership moved from one to the other. We had one focus, one goal. What could we do to make this day as his parents would have it. Especially Beth, the minister's daughter, who had tradition and ceremony in her blood. The funeral took place on a Saturday in January. The weather was magnificent, sunny and cool—a sweater or blazer was all that was needed.

Some of his closest friends spoke. They were young men between twenty-five and thirty. They were open-hearted. They cried. They told stories that brought me right into Phillip. Their egos were tucked away. They were image-less. They described things they had done with Phillip. They described things they had learned from Phillip. They described Phillip. They did not leave out the fact he did dangerous things and explored forbidden boundaries.

I didn't know what to think. I would gladly have seen either of my daughters married to any of these young men. I was proud to have been part of their lives, even a small part. How could an organization I look upon with such lack of pride have produced such wonderful men? Perhaps genes are everything. Perhaps they were badly damaged by the way they were raised, but strong enough to figure out how to live productively.

I was truly taken aback by these young men. It made me think how different we all really were in spite of the fact Synanon the organization was fairly stable in the way it manipulated and controlled us. I always say that Synanon was a mostly bad organization with mostly good people. When I saw these men, I thought about the good people part. All the women who gave all they had to raising them. All the men who took them on as apprentices and surrogate sons and younger brothers. All the parents who may not have spent enough time, but loved them nevertheless. Who may have been misguided, but were not mean or abusive. And I thought about the relationships some of the people who were raised in Synanon have with one another, the love they so unashamedly expressed.

We had much practice putting ourselves aside so we could work for Synanon, do what was asked of us unquestioningly. That practice came in handy when we actually had a cause that was for the moment bigger than we were. It felt good to be with each other in that way again. We all felt it.

I think Synanon is finally becoming simply a part of my life. It no longer defines me. It no longer seems big and overpowering, and I no longer feel overpowered by it. I have reclaimed much of my own power, and the more powerful I feel the more I am able to see Synanon as but one segment of my life. I do not want to take the good and leave the bad, but I do want to be able to see I had both good and bad experiences and that just because I was taken by it for so long does not mean I am forever damaged and diminished. There is power in my being able to see Synanon as I now do, and the clearer I see it, the clearer I see the people I've known for over thirty years, the more I am able to respect their strengths as well as see their weaknesses.

I think the whole experience with Phillip moved me over another bit. While there is value in looking at experiences, people and events under a microscope, there is equal value in stepping way back so that you can also see the sky.

194

PART V
LEAVING AND LOOKING BACK

1. LEAVING

2. NO PAST REGRETS OR FUTURE FEARS

3. POWER AND RANK

4. THE GIFT OF DEPRESSION

5. PUTTING RELATIONSHIPS IN ORDER

6. POSTSCRIPTS ON CICILY

7. THE DECISION TO LEAVE

8. RE-ENTERING THE LARGER COMMUNITY

9. ABOUT EVIL

10. EX-ADDICTS

11. GUILT AND SHAME

12. DIRECT CONTACT WITH CHUCK

13. CYCLES

LEAVING

When first asked what made me leave Synanon, I thought of the last thing that happened, the event that made me say to Jerry as he walked through the door, "Let's move to San Diego. Second Market is opening a small subsidiary in San Diego, and Mary and Vannie are moving down. Let's you and me and Elyse go, too. This solves all our problems."

Elyse was graduating from eighth grade and her prospects in the small high school she was destined for were unpromising. I had been searching for a solution and feeling almost hopeless, and then *voila!*—San Diego.

For months, perhaps even years, I couldn't see any more than the final part of my leaving process. I left Synanon because I needed to get Elyse in a decent high school. Now I realize this event came at the end of about three years of leaving. I will try to follow that thread in spite of the fact it is knotted and twisted and in no way a neatly wrapped up ball of yarn.

There are two elements presently in my life that were absent in Synanon, two elements I have cultivated diligently over the past ten years: they are substance and abundance. I hope the descriptions I now write about demonstrate how I began the process of building those elements into my life several years before I actually left.

NO PAST REGRETS OR FUTURE FEARS

The years from changing partners to the time of Sarah's ordeal, (1976–1983 approximately) were quiescent years for me in terms of my consciousness and conscience. I had made the pivotal decision, at the exact moment I heard about Paul's beating, to turn my head to not even catch a glimpse of a side of Synanon that I did not want to have to think about. I was powerless to do anything about that darker side of Synanon and didn't want to learn anything that would start me down a path that could only have led me to consider leaving.

I was rather Red Guard in Synanon. It was easier to follow the party line. Find out what the current thought was, figure out a way to make it mine and spit it out with the rest of my ilk at dinner tables and in games. First, I thought this was surely the road to eternal acceptance, and second, it was easier than engaging in thoughts that could only lead me where I did not want to go.

I was a very good girl in Synanon. I did my aerobics religiously, wore my silver dollar around my neck for the required period we had to do that, never ate sugar, wore my overalls, clipped my hair and spread the gospel according to Chuck. Not everyone was as conscientious as I was, but I think the people I hung around most of the time were. This was my choice, but I had lots of help from a system based upon unquestioning loyalty and complete trust in the leadership genius of Chuck.

I do not accept the idea that I acted as I did solely to garner acceptance. I also know I am not without curiosity and an almost unquenchable thirst to understand the motivations of people. My silence was part of a larger system that demanded the kind of acquiescence I so willingly participated in. One of the things that fostered it was the constant admonition to live in the present. Place one foot firmly in front of the other. One day at a time. No past regrets or future fears.

"No past regrets or future fears" was repeated almost as often as "please let me first and always examine myself." Any expression of either future fears or past regrets was immediately squashed. Our pasts consisted of all that came before Synanon which was simply bad, and all ex-addicts were reminded of these pasts when they expressed any discontent with life in Synanon. They were unequivocally told if they left they would "fall down a manhole." All references to the future were to assure us over and over that "some day" we would all be rich, that the "net" would be there to catch us when we needed it, and that as long as we stayed in Synanon we would have security. The future was gossamer, light and airy and always just beyond our reach.

I cannot tell you how many times people wanted to talk about issues that were vitally important and were shut up by the entire game. The death of parents, marriages that ended, children leaving were all pushed aside. It was commonplace for someone to begin to talk about truly compelling issues, and another person to say something like, "I don't think that's what really has you upset. I think your feelings have more to do with the fact you didn't get invited to the Home Place party last Saturday night. Let's talk about that." And the entire game would gravitate to what was utterly trivial. Hard to believe, but mind-numbingly typical. We were always brought firmly into the present moment, and as Synanon shrunk and our world became smaller and smaller there were fewer and fewer issues to distract us from the really meaningful issues of our lives.

Future and past figure heavily into the present. Having cancer has crystallized the importance of future, for when I realized one of the ways I might fight recurrence was to visualize a big, bright future filled with plans that were real and meaningful, I found myself pretty rusty. This inability to think far into my future troubled me and led me to examine more about life in Synanon, where we had

198

no milestones. We didn't celebrate birthdays. We didn't celebrate anniversaries. Every once in a while such a party would break through the strict discipline and all hell would break loose. No graduations. No celebration of the individual. We did attempt to invent our own ceremonies and celebrations, and for a long time the possibility in doing that, in breathing new life into what I perceived as tired traditions, inspired me and captured my imagination. We threw a couple of big, group, theme weddings. We established monthly birthday parties for the kids born in that particular month, but still allowed no presents. The invention of our own ceremonies fell short. They failed in the way ceremony and tradition and celebration are supposed to anchor and form roots. They did not contain the elements of celebration and ceremony—repetition and rote and formality and history—the kinds of tradition that bring both hope and promise.

The quiescence during the years between changing partners and Sarah's leaving began to unravel in the mid-eighties. The unraveling was not linear and I cannot tell in what order the spiral into my exit from Synanon took place. I am certain my marriage to Jerry, which by this time was about five years old, had centered me in a way I'd never been centered before, had helped me move more and more toward my center of gravity. In addition, Synanon was beginning to come undone because Chuck was drinking, which served to push his manic states out to the edge. I recall my everyday thoughts were being invaded by small points of light from deep within myself. The fact Synanon didn't celebrate milestones like birthdays and anniversaries and graduations began to grate on me, and I readily admitted to myself I believed something essentially wrong with these absences. Issues I'd passed off as trivial, as obstacles toward my becoming a better Synanon person, as resistance to change, persisted in calling my energy to them.

When Synanon had been vibrant with a population that formed a critical mass, it was easy to stay in the present. Our lives were being toyed with on the most intimate levels. We had a lot to deal with. Changes were constant. What we ate, where we slept, who was taking care of our children, where we worked and lived were continually being manipulated. The present easily absorbed our full attention. But as we shrunk, that changed.

I recently held a wedding for Elyse and her new husband at my house. We planned the wedding for a full year, and it was particularly challenging because we were uniting two families that were culturally different. I wanted everybody to have a good time, and I knew that it was going to be a tricky manipulation. I might add when they said they wanted a traditional wedding, I was horrified. It took them a full year to wear me down and once they succeeded, I began having a lot of fun with the celebration. The wedding was a monumental success. I had the best time I've ever had. The kids said it far exceeded their expectations. In addition to the main event, Max and Elyse's stepmother had a small reception in the town where they live, and her husband's parents had a big party for their very large family, in the town they live. We have been to all the parties. A friend made a precious video of the kids growing up along with parts of the wedding. We have the professional photos, and I have a scrapbook of other photos, including all the parties and her bridal shower. It was a joyous celebration and I hope to enjoy the photos and video for many years. I also hope to celebrate many more such happy events.

POWER AND RANK

People in Synanon were given vast amounts of power over others for a variety of reasons. Cicily had power by virtue of her being Chuck's daughter and wielding the Dederich name. She also was vested with the power of position as the chairman of Synanon. The game was the only organizational system of checks and balances, and the game became more and more corrupted as time went on. One marker of the corruption of the game was when the people involved in "protecting" Synanon held a contract to never discuss their activities or feelings about those activities in games. It was easy to abuse power in Synanon and we all did it. I'd venture a guess most people left when they could no longer handle some kind of abuse they were experiencing.

These abuses happened in small as well as large ways. Invasions came at the dinner table as well as in the game. One of mine came in a large jacuzzi.

In addition to hating my hair, I have a pot belly. I have always had a pot belly. Until I was fifty, I weighed between one-hundred-and-five and one-hundred-and-ten pounds. I am five-feet-two-inches small and relatively well proportioned. But in the way women have of magnifying the minor, that pot always seemed immense to me. If God had really loved me he would have given me good hair and a concave belly.

Jerry and I lived at the Home Place in the early eighties. By this time Marin County had successfully ousted us—and everybody lived in Central California—in one of two facilities; the Home Place where Chuck and Sharon and a small population of about seventy people lived and the Strip which was seven miles up into the foothills of the Sierras where everyone else lived. It was exquisitely beautiful land—hills and trees and pristine air. Sequoia National Forest was only a few miles away.

Standing beside the pool under a large gazebo at the Home Place was a big redwood jacuzzi. This area was just outside the Lodge, which was the main gathering hall, to which Chuck and Sharon's residence was attached. A bit below, but near the pool, were two double-wide mobile homes where Cicily and her husband, and Chuck's chief attorney and his wife lived. Anyone who lived at the Home Place or was visiting as a guest could use the jacuzzi any time they wanted. Chuck was usually out there at about 4:00 PM and people would join him. After sundown it was customary to soak in the nude, and most evenings small groups of men and women gathered to soak and swim without bathing suits.

One cool evening just before spring, Jerry and I were hanging out in the Lodge in front of a roaring fire and, looking through the patio doors, noticed there were people in the soak tub. We decided to join them. We removed our clothing in the small bathrooms nearby and joined the others. The water was very hot, over one-hundred-and-ten degrees. After a while, feeling cooked, I raised myself out of the tank and sat on the generous wooden rim. There were still people in the water and others were seated on the rim along with me. I sat with my arm casually flung over my belly, as over the years I have perfected the habit of trying to cover it up either with clothing or an arm or book or blanket or just about anything handy. I am conflicted over this preoccupation that I believe is an indulgence because I am actually blessed with a well functioning and attractive vessel.

Cicily, sitting opposite me, took notice of the arm over the belly and was compelled to offer me some sisterly advice. "Alice, move your hand. I've been watching you and you always cover your belly. You have this great body, and you always cover your belly. Why do you do that? I don't understand. It doesn't make any sense." As she said this she looked to the others for support.

My face turned hot. I did not respond, except to move my arm, which felt like a piece of lead, exposing what felt to be a giant protrusion. I told myself what she said was in a way a compliment. Yes? Cicily could say anything. She probably thought she was speaking to me intimately. But all I felt was exposed. I wish I had known eventually I would get my turn to pull the rug from under her in the not too distant future, and I was soon to take back the power I had relinquished years ago.

There were many ways people took advantage of their power and rank. To some degree we all engaged in kicking the person below because that is what we were taught by the people who were supposed to be our role models. But not too much attention was paid to the average person's power abuse because we were all absorbed in nursing our own various injustices from the power elite. I certainly never saw myself as an abusive person and was much too busy looking over my own shoulder for any self-examination about my own behavior.

A few years ago an old friend told me of my own engagement in this power hierarchy when she reminded me of a negative evaluation I'd written of her work performance when I had been her supervisor in the school. These things can be so subtle. I'd all but forgotten about it, but to her, the evaluation, which she discovered when she went through her personnel file just before she left Synanon, was like a punch in the stomach, especially because it was I who had written it.

She was one of the women who had devoted her life to tirelessly caring for the young children and gave love and warmth freely and unselfishly. She had also devoted herself to my daughter, Julie, and made sure she was welcomed with a bed and bulletin board each time she visited. She did this for years, and because time with children was always her first priority, chores and errands and paper work came last, which meant she usually worked overtime in order to accomplish everything required of her.

The major thrust of my evaluation was I declared her a minimal employee. I chose to base her evaluation on the fact that she had difficulty completing chores. Only after thinking about it for quite a while was I able to understand I did this for several reasons. First and most obviously because I thought it identified me with whoever would be reading the evaluation. (It probably was never read.) See, I have Synanon's economic interest at heart. See, I am more efficient than she is. I knew no one would care that she made up stories every evening to help children fall asleep, and that she'd stop everything to listen to a child's discovery or a disagreement, and when all else failed she'd rub a restless child's back forever until he or she was calm enough for sleep—leaving her shift hours after it officially ended. So I declared her minimal in her performance.

Digging a little deeper, I can see she had been able to do something I was not capable of, since she had a warmth and generosity of spirit I did not yet possess. Because I was unable to demonstrate these qualities at the time, I devalued them to the point they were not even a consideration in my evaluation of her work. When she reminded me of the letter, I offered an embarrassed apology.

I believe Synanon was built upon such a hierarchy of abusive power. The server in the food line gave you more than you wanted, the supervisor evaluated a subordinate unjustly to gain favor, a school demonstrator set up impossible goals for a teenager, a newcomer demanded a little child help her with a chore. From top to bottom such power plays were a part of our daily interactions.

THE GIFT OF DEPRESSION

I have been depressed much of my life. My depressions are relatively moderate; some positive energy inside my body is replaced with these buzzing, winged demons that spread dullness and hopelessness throughout. Sometimes they form a solid mass, and sometimes they fly in small groups intermittently spreading their darkness. I know they are there because I become irritable, impatient and frustrated. In addition to the winged demons, I provide housing for tiny, hyperactive gnomes who jump around filling me with anxiety. I'm never going to get this done. Never. I just don't have enough time. I ruminate, unable to concentrate on the task at hand. These two creatures wear me down and fatigue fills me to the point of dread. Light fades and sound becomes muted.

I have carried these demons with me since childhood and now that finally the light and sound shine through, I often wonder at what I might have accomplished had I not spent so much energy fighting the darkness.

Depression masks true emotion. It is a defense mechanism. It makes me furious when psychologists say they don't believe in antidepressants. I'm certain the therapists who take this stand have clearly never been depressed or lived close to someone who was. Antidepressants put the demons to sleep so you can pay attention to what's really going on. It's something like Synanon. We were so caught up in the change of the moment we couldn't think about past and future and build independent lives. Depression is very compelling. It doesn't allow you to think about anything other than the gloom undulating inside you. Medication can relieve the pain so that you can deal with underlying issues. The problem as I see it is when people rely only on the antidepressants and do not do the work of getting to the underlying issues.

The end of Synanon came in similar fashion to the beginning. First, there had been my attraction to the conversion process, which inspired me to believe I could change. Then bit by bit I was sucked into the authoritarianism and control Chuck wielded over all of us, thinking with each mandate I was making a small sacrifice in light of changing people and changing the world. Had I a stronger sense of myself, this probably would not have happened, and like thousands of others I would have walked away.

The newcomer program that anchored me to the inspirational and spiritual part of Synanon dwindled to a very small and relatively unimportant segment of the community. By the mid-seventies, Synanon's primary focus was on developing its business and fighting the many lawsuits it was accruing. The advertising specialties business and law offices pulled on most of Synanon's energies. Little else was going on that was educational, nourishing or even entertaining by the mid-eighties.

At that time my depression manifested itself in two ways. First irritability, frustration and hopelessness became exaggerated, and I felt a constant anxiety buzzing around my chest and head. The targets of these feelings were primarily physical things. Jerry and I lived in a mobile home, the one we shared with the couple whose child ran away, which was a few hundred yards from the shed on the Strip property in Central California. The path from the home to the shed was unpaved and poorly lighted with potholes scattered here and there. After it rained puddles formed in the potholes, and in the darkness I invariably stepped in one, soaking one foot or the other or both on my way to the shed. This just set me off. It seemed intolerable that the walk was unlit and full of wet holes. Unacceptable. Seedy. Substandard. It was a metaphor for what my life had become. I was knocked off my goal, the simple one of getting to the shed for dinner. I had to return home and change my shoes and socks. Since I only had one pair of dress shoes, one pair of flats, one pair of running shoes, one pair of knock around shoes, I might very well have to change my outfit as well. Knocked off course for nothing. It drove me crazy.

Elyse, Vannie and Tamara lived in a long, narrow bunkhouse. A porch was lined with rooms of varying sizes, and a shower room and toilet room were in the center. Since the girls were the youngest, they got to shower last. Several times a week, I went over during showers because as Synanon became more and more meaningless, spending time with the kids became more and more important to me, and I often hung out with the girls as they dried and dressed. The school had by this time become insignificant with little staff, so we mothers spent a good part of each day supervising the girls who were about nine. They were incredibly sweet children, rarely complained, whined or asked for anything and loved spending time with any of the assorted mothers they owned.

The kids had the chicken sheets, towels and bathmats I spoke of before. They were red, yellow, black and white, and we called them chicken sheets, towels, etc. because they were dotted with pictures of large chickens. It was a pattern we all tired of quickly, and they were cheap, undernourished linens. I walked into the shower room to find the girls huddled together on soaking wet bathmats with the scrawny towels pulled tightly around their shivering bodies. The hot water had run out. I was beside myself. The old me would have laughed at the downside of being the youngest kids in a children's community and concluded they were fine, just fine. Nothing wrong with a little ruggedness. A small sacrifice in light of the great gift of being raised in Synanon. But by this time, I was appalled and could think only of soft, plush bathmats, steamy bathrooms and fat, oversized towels, at least two, one for their heads and one to drown their bodies in.

I felt despair that I couldn't put a nail into the wall of the prefabricated homes I had lived in for the past four or so years; they just fell through. I couldn't hang pictures. I hated the food which was heavy with salt and ate mostly salads. By the mid-eighties we were once again eating sugar, and hair was any length we wanted, and I thought it was cheap and institutional that we only had desserts once a week. Why couldn't we have desserts four times a week? Why couldn't we have fruit? Dissatisfaction with seemingly small things became overwhelming.

One of the things that disturbed me more and more were the drinking parties that for years had been practically the only form of entertainment available to us. Most of us believed Chuck started drinking in 1978, although I've heard he was seen drinking much earlier in a bar near Tomales Bay, which he drove to on his motorcycle. But when he began drinking publicly in Synanon, he introduced alcohol as part of the Synanon lifestyle. Chuck wanted drinking buddies, but of course had to couch his personal needs in some vision. By this time things were so screwed up in Synanon,

I am embarrassed to even say this, but he declared, probably in a drunken stupor, ex-addicts could drink alcohol because Synanon was a controlled environment. They could drink safely within the community.

The sober squad was invented, and each week at parties where alcohol flowed freely, six or eight people remained sober to watch the flock. If you were on sober squad you could send people home who were obviously out of control, you drove anyone who wished to be driven, you tidied up the dining room, and cleaned up vomit and sometimes even worse when a person got really out of hand, which they did from time to time. One man used to sit with a water glass filled with vodka at parties and drank to excess at other times as well. Synanon became dotted with many thinly disguised alcoholics. After my early attempts to drink myself into some kind of high failed, I hated the parties and left as early as I possibly could get away. I stayed away from drunks when I was on sober squad and spent a lot of time busing dishes and nibbling at the desserts others weren't interested in.

The kids were allowed to come to these "family" parties at the Strip, and I've been told the teenagers found their way into the liquor closets and took what they wanted for their own little parties. As one might predict, there were a lot of people in Synanon who simply could not handle alcohol. They could not have one drink, or two, or three and then stop. One young woman just went nuts when she drank. She was in her early twenties and had come into Synanon as a child with her addicted mother. Her name was Jean, and she was young enough to know all the kids. Because they were kids, and she paid attention to them, they looked up to her.

Elyse must have been eleven years old when, the morning after a party, she told me, "Last night Jean was dancing all by herself

209

on the dance floor and she pulled her dress up over her head. She was drunk."

Once again, I found myself furious.

"She probably was. Some people should not drink and Jean is one of those people. They just can't seem to stop drinking when they should and then they get drunk and do dumb things."

What I was thinking was a great deal more compelling. If I didn't live in Synanon, I would never have a person like Jean in my home. If I didn't live in Synanon, I would never even go to such a party. If I didn't live in Synanon, I would protect my child from such behavior and try to introduce her to "fun" that had a bit more substance to it than a bunch of people getting sloshed and having conversations in slurred speech they later described as intimate.

I was in the process of constructing my future out of Synanon.

When rumors started the IRS was going to put liens on a fund most of us had our savings in, I started moving money out of Synanon, even though we were assured over and over the money was safe. It wasn't, and after Jerry and I left with our money, some people lost substantial amounts when the fund was indeed attached. I pictured a house with real closets and real walls I could hang real pictures on, not the $20.00 posters I bought at Gottschalks department store— encased in plastic and framed by some lightweight, gold-painted tin. I saw perfect towels that soaked up water and bathmats that were so absorbent they hardly got wet even after you dripped puddles on them.

When we did leave, Jerry and I took Elyse to shows and movies and bookstores and we bought music and played it all the time, encouraging interests that would teach her entertainment entailed more than swallowing as much alcohol as you could get your hands on.

I believe that my depression gave me the metaphors and pictures I needed to move me into a future beyond Synanon, and it was because of those metaphors I knew what I needed to do after I left.

PUTTING RELATIONSHIPS IN ORDER

I was not the only person suffering from depression, and Chuck, who was taking antidepressants, strongly promoted their use. He basically got those of us in distress quieted down, but the drug I took turned out to be a good one for me because it enabled me to make some necessary changes.

The best thing about reorganizing my life after antidepressants quieted the dark energy inside me, was I cut loose certain things. I stopped going to the Super Games at the Home Place, which were games held in a large room containing video equipment. These games were broadcast live on Home Place TV and also recorded so they could be sent over to the Strip as each reel ended. The Super Game had become the place from which much of Synanon's business was managed. They were orchestrated, and the executive committee was assigned to watch them and patch in through a telephone system when they had a point to make. Chuck and Sharon listened, and although Chuck was forbidden to play the game or have anything to do with the running of Synanon as terms of his probation in the rattlesnake case, his voice could be heard as he told his wife, Sharon, what he wanted her to say.

Marriages were broken up both in and out of the game, because

Chuck determined that one member of a couple or another was "inappropriate." People were fired from jobs in Synanon and sent out of the community to find work, and others were fined for minor infractions. One time a woman was fined for alleged rudeness. Jerry, in Texas on a business trip, was in a hotel room late one evening with some Synanon people who had been drinking. The conversation became loud, and someone called security who came to the room and asked them to be quiet. The person who had made the call was also from Synanon but didn't realize the noise was coming from other Synanon people. When she got home, mustering all the self-righteousness she could manage, which was an inordinate amount, she gamed them about their inappropriate behavior and the fact that their loud drunkenness could tarnish the name of Synanon, which they represented.

Jerry was fined $500.00 because he hadn't stopped the loud people. Jerry is about as mild mannered as they come and the idea of his being fined for participating in drunken loudness was ridiculous. Jerry never got drunk. He was as furious as he was able to be and began thinking about leaving. The fine was just one thing in a series of indignities that rankled. His business opinions, which in the real world have made it possible for us to live well and for me to write, were not being taken seriously. He felt most of the current business moves were poorly thought out—even dangerously stupid. He no longer knew what he was doing in Synanon, and the only reason he did not say anything to me was because he was not certain how I would react. Often, when people confessed to thinking about leaving, the group pushed them toward making an immediate decision. Get off the fence. He was not prepared to end his relationship with Synanon as well as his marriage and relationship with Elyse and Julie.

Although Jerry and I were deeply attached by this time, we

had never discussed the fact that our allegiance to Synanon had dramatically changed and our connection to one another was greater than our connection to the community. This had been a major shift in both of us, but this kind of conversation was absolutely off limits to people like Jerry and me. It was off limits between me and myself. Again, any thought that might lead to an examination of whether or not to stay was still too dangerous for either of us. We were unable to be honest with each other past a certain point because any kind of negativity was still threatening. Even friendships were tentative. You knew if your closest friend got in trouble, a "jackpot," you would keep a prudent distance, walking the thin line that made you appear to be on the side of the prosecutor (Synanon) while trying to hold some degree of compassion for the person undergoing the object lesson. In other words, a jackpot meant abandonment, even if it was temporary, and talking about leaving could lead to a jackpot.

In hindsight I think I would have ultimately left had Jerry decided he had to go at that time, but I can also see myself bringing the issue into a game and putting the decision in the hands of the community. I might have allowed Jerry to become the "bad guy." I might have even been deemed a bad wife, the reason Jerry was really unhappy, and the community might have talked us into a separation. *Get rid of her, Jerry. She's the problem. Your life will improve the minute you get with someone else.* For all of the disrespect Jerry felt, his basic skills were needed and used. His skills translated into hard, cold cash and I was far less valuable in that way. We simply weren't quite ready to leave, but the $500.00 fine went a long way toward eroding Jerry's appreciation of Synanon.

It was in the late eighties that things came to a head for me in terms of my relationships. There were more law cases in Synanon than

213

most people could keep track of. We, in the general population, got snatches of information from time to time, announcements before lunch or dinner when we were all gathered, TV news reports that were then interpreted for us by our legal staff, and less frequently from conversations with people who worked on the cases. The official word, either from Cicily or the legal staff, was always in the form of a pep talk ending with some shouted slogan like, "We'll never, never, ever, ever quit," or "We'll get the bastards," or "They'll never get us," or some fiery cheer. We were also lied to about the outcomes of case settlements, told we "won," when in fact we "settled," with money paid out.

One evening everyone was in the dining room of the Strip property and had just been given a general account of the law cases. We then broke up into small groups. Jerry and I went with Cicily and one of the lawyers into the living room. At this time there were about four hundred people living in Synanon and about three hundred lived at the Strip. The living room was dimly lit and uninviting in spite of the massive fireplace, a community project built in hopes of making the immense room cozier. About fifty of us were seated on couches, chairs brought in from the dining room, folding chairs and the floor.

The format was question and answer. Jerry asked a sincere question about one of the cases that had been mentioned earlier to the larger group. It was not a bullshit question designed to elicit an answer that would make everyone feel good, it was a genuine question asking for some details.

Cicily took it upon herself to respond. "I'm glad, Jerry Rost, that you're not important enough to testify on behalf of Synanon in any of these cases because you don't have the balls it takes to speak on behalf of Synanon."

Something snapped, my gut churned and I got up to walk toward the bathroom. I don't think I've ever felt such rage. I paced back and forth in the small bathroom, composed myself and returned, managing to stay until the end and walk up the hill to our module before I exploded into a thousand lightning rods of anger.

When we entered the bedroom I began pacing and yelling.

"Who does that ignorant bitch think she is, talking to you like that? I'm not going to live this way anymore. I'm not going to stand for that kind of bad manners anymore. I don't want to be around people like that. This is no way to live. This is ridiculous. Who is she? Who does she think she is? She is nothing. No one." Neither of us had ever spoken badly of any officer of Synanon, so my outburst was new in nature. I went on and on unable to diffuse the rage, and he reluctantly agreed I might have a point. He just couldn't figure out how it was going to be possible to live in Synanon and have nothing to do with Cicily.

Jerry has a hard time with anger and hostility. He never used to allow it. Now he recognizes such feelings and can even express them, but it is almost funny to watch—kind of like a little kid practicing. I have to be very careful not to laugh because it diffuses his anger which is not something I want to do. Or maybe I do, but I don't.

I asked Cicily's secretary to let her know I wanted a game with her. Several days later, Cicily held a meeting for parents to talk about the school. It was a bullshit meeting. Cicily was telling everybody how great the school was, how great the kids were, and everybody nodded in agreement. I sat there wondering how they could be so blind to the fact the teenagers were wandering around this tiny community, no stimulation, no friends, no dating, being taught by

215

one teacher. Jesus, they were in prison. At least the little girls had us and we chauffeured them around to gymnastics class, summer camp; and they, unlike the teenagers, were in public school so they had school activities. After the meeting, in which we were seated in a circle, she invited us to play the game if we wanted to.

"Alice, I understand you want to play the game with me. Now's as good a time as any."

I was taken aback, but did not waste one moment playing the game in the way I had originally believed it was intended, as if I had nothing to lose, because by this time, I was beginning to realize I had nothing to lose because Synanon no longer meant much to me. It took me all of a second to bring forth the same fierce rage I'd felt the evening she'd publicly attacked Jerry.

"If you ever, ever open your big mouth and talk to my husband the way you did the other night, I am going to embarrass you as you have never been embarrassed in your entire life. I don't know who the hell you think you are, you ignorant, uneducated, spoiled know-nothing, but don't you ever speak to me or my husband or my child in any but the most polite way—ever again—in any setting. *Do you understand?*"

There was a raw force behind my words that came from a place of protection deep within. Cicily had been rude to me time after time, but her behavior toward Jerry was what snapped me. I could see Cicily visibly fold back into her chair, her mouth went soft with disbelief, and her eyes faded as she retreated to a place she hardly ever experienced in public. I had made a hit, a direct hit. And it felt great.

The next day Cicily apologized to Jerry, but this was a tired habit of hers. These apologies were supposed to be some kind of grand gesture of humility from the royal princess that would make

216

everything okay. And we were supposed to be grateful for being in a community in which someone of so much importance could apologize with such grace. Then she would do the same thing again and again.

Cicily asked me if I still wanted to be in a game with her and I said yes. She invited Jerry and me to a couples' game several days later.

I told her, "You can take your apology and stuff it up your ass. It isn't good enough for me. The fact that you think you can EVER speak like that to ANYONE out of a game is the problem."

Her husband asked me, "Alice, don't you ever get so frustrated that you lose it. Are you so perfect all the time?"

I answered I didn't lose it like that, not ever.

Cicily told me, "You are a bottomless pit. That's your problem. Nothing is ever good enough. This is a waste of time."

Most of the people in the game began to *tut, tut* at my inability to accept her apology, including, I might add, my husband—but I didn't care what anybody said, and their dismissal of me had no impact whatsoever. It's amazing when you understand yourself, the impact of others' misunderstanding is so diminished. I was finished with any pretense of devotion to Cicily because, although I couldn't recognize it at the time, I was formulating a new sense of what was meaningful. It was becoming clear to me ideas and visions and philosophies were interesting, but what happens between people is what really matters.

POSTSCRIPTS ON CICILY

Cicily had really gotten under my skin in Synanon, and I chose

217

to project a lot of my negative feelings upon her after I left. She was my target, just as other members of the executive committee were chosen by other people as targets for their anger. Interestingly, few people found Chuck an easy target for their hostility.

How do I feel about Cicily now? Many of my feelings are resolved in the way such things resolve themselves bit by bit, small shifts that bring forth clearer and clearer pictures of the relationship. Today from a distance I see three Cicilys.

Mostly I see the eleven-year-old child, slightly rounded, with thick, brown curls holding her baby brother while her mother loads groceries into their car in a parking lot. I wonder if she saw her stepfather approach (with gun in hand) and I try to imagine what she felt as she, entering her own womanhood, watched her beautiful mother lose her life in the space of one breath. In a perfectly ordinary moment this extraordinary thing happened that would forever change her and forever secure her into that moment. It sickens me so little attention was paid by her father or our community to this monumental instant in her life.

I see a woman who was probably more abused by her father than was any other single person in Synanon. I can never know this for certain because rarely, if ever, were the personal humiliations suffered at his hand exposed, but her horrible manners and abusive behavior must surely have grown from her own mistreatment. Had she been nourished and loved, it is likely she would have been nourishing and loving.

And finally, I still feel some small degree of humiliation that I allowed this relationship to persist for so many years, that I allowed my intellect to be so diminished, and that I allowed my instincts to be squashed. I handed over my power. I allowed her anger to swallow me, and that is hard to admit. Perhaps that is why people find it so difficult to share these stories.

THE DECISION TO LEAVE

In spite of all the energy I'd expended trying to be loyal and committed, my decision to leave was simple and totally undramatic. More and more of my inner life consisted of the construction of a life separate from what Synanon offered me. More and more of my conscious thought rejected what I was being told by the officers of Synanon. I supported individual choices that conflicted with communal philosophy, like Max's setting up a trust fund for Elyse's education and determining what of his salary he was going to donate to Synanon instead of continuing to allow those decisions to rest with the executives. A peer of mine decided to keep an inheritance instead of donating it. Once, when this woman was opening a Synanon facility in Chicago and had been asked by Synanon to visit large businesses to procure things needed for the new house, she'd asked Synanon to forward her money to buy a winter coat and a dress. She was allowed the winter coat, but not the dress. I saluted her decision to never have to be in a situation like that again. More and more of my time was spent with my children, husband and closest friends. I was on the sales team and loved getting away from Synanon, but hated sales. I hated traveling and being away from Jerry and Elyse and Julie, but I was happy to leave Synanon and the rhetoric. In spite of all these changes, Jerry and I still did not talk about leaving.

Synanon was crumbling. Chuck was sequestered away at the Home Place and acting totally insane. I, fortunately, had no direct experience of him during that period. It was truly an *Emperor's New Clothes* fiasco. Chuck was in the throes of a manic episode that

219

included sexually inappropriate behavior and insane mandates, like when he insisted everyone in Synanon use only one plate for their entire meal, or that we all sew pockets on all of the shirts we wore to work. We had to have one pocket over each breast, and carry sixteen-ounce containers of water at all times.

One afternoon he insisted his eyeglasses had been moved. They were not in the exact spot he had left them. He felt like he had been raped, personally invaded. He ranted and raved over the "wire" for a long time insisting the culprit come forward. Then he called everyone together, including all of the teenagers, and had them break into groups and game all through the night about rape and personal invasion. It was summer and Mary, Beatrice and I along with our lucky husbands were visiting the girls in summer camp near Yosemite so we missed it. But when we returned, we were scooped by a couple of directors who told us what a meaningful experience it had been. His executive committee stood by him. Others in the community were not so sure.

Business decisions were being made that were dangerous, and they were being made by people who were drinking heavily and constantly. Jerry, who was one of a handful of people who could actually read and analyze a financial statement, saw that the business was quickly heading for ruin. There was a lot of talk about money. The executives were paid extravagant salaries plus all expenses were taken care of by Synanon, and the salespeople, some doing over a million dollars in sales a year, were disgruntled. They wanted more pay. They wanted better food. Jerry felt the salespeople were going to leave, break away and form their own business. He is a problem solver and organized a group—key salesmen, investors, and others who were not in management—to meet with the executive committee. In a fiery and unpleasant meeting they made a series of demands. They asked for the resignations of the entire executive committee because Synanon was headed for economic ruin under their leadership. They demanded Synanon cease paying for all of Chuck's alcohol. The executive committee resigned, a temporary board was put in place and a committee was appointed to come up with a reorganization plan for Synanon. We all felt we owned Synanon. We all had to take responsibility for fixing whatever was wrong. Leaving, to those of us who still remained, continued to ring of failure and excommunication.

I had pretty much moved beyond my anxiety and depression and was doing well at engaging in activities that made me feel good while trying to ignore the rest of what was going on in Synanon. But I became anxious because Elyse's eighth grade graduation was fast approaching and the public school she was scheduled to attend was simply unacceptable. My alternatives were highly unwieldy, and I was seriously concerned. Two lawyers from the law office had moved to San Francisco with their wives and Synanon's blessing. There was a lot of movement and talk about the future of Synanon. Several people were talking about having babies, getting vasectomies reversed. Things were changing quickly.

Mary called me one Saturday afternoon to tell me that she was going to move to San Diego with her husband and Vannie. A subsidiary of one of Synanon's smaller businesses was moving a portion of its office to that city and Mary's husband worked for that office. I hung up the phone in shock. At first I felt betrayed; Mary hadn't even asked me what I thought. But within seconds I realized there was no point in staying in Central California without Mary and Vannie.

Jerry walked through the door shortly after the call.

"Listen, Jerry, I have big news. Mary and Larry and Vannie are moving to San Diego with a group of people from Second Market. Let's go too."

"You mean leave Synanon?"

"Well, not exactly. There will be about fifty of us down there. Elyse can go to a big city high school where she might actually learn something. We can still work for Synanon since we can sell from anywhere. Besides, I feel like I am going to get sick again. I am feeling more and more anxious when I am home, and I don't like being on the road. Things are really nutty here. Won't it be nice to live in a city again? To have our own place?"

One of the reasons Jerry moved into Synanon is he has the most difficult time making big decisions. He moved into Synanon at a time when he was trying to decide between two jobs shortly after finishing graduate school. Each offered excellent opportunities for a young man starting his career, and he simply could not make the choice. Synanon was a way of avoiding that choice. His entire countenance relaxed when I introduced the conversation about moving to San Diego. His face, usually calm, relaxed even more and I could see the light of optimism and enthusiasm slowly reignite. This was a decision he was ready to accept help in making.

"Who's going to cook? Are you going to cook every night?"

"We'll work it out."

We did not actually think we were leaving Synanon. It was more like we were moving in a direction dictated by the changing needs of the residents. It took almost another year for the people remaining to realize Synanon was disintegrating—at least physically disintegrating. It died a long, hard death.

RE-ENTERING THE LARGER COMMUNITY

In some ways San Diego was culture shock, and in others it seemed I was back home after having taken a short detour. In looking back over the last ten years, I have to say Jerry and I had a relatively easy time of it. Our lives unfolded with seeming ease. We came to San Diego with a truck filled with nothing in particular, boxes and boxes of I don't know what because we did not own a dish or fork, bed or chair. We moved four times in seven years, fulfilled all of my material needs and more, found a dream house, educated one fine young woman, brought a second one deeply into our lives, built a model business, got two dogs and put money away for our old age.

The hard part was all under the surface. We hadn't a clue as to how much money we needed to live, or what we needed to feel like we were living well, and for the first six months watched the flow of money as if it was a precious fluid. We never ate a meal out, and when we finally went out for pizza, didn't order Cokes because they were so expensive. We also didn't know how we wanted to live regarding the making of money. Did we want to build a big business or keep it small, manage several sales people or have Jerry be the only salesman, travel a little or a lot, travel only in California or all over the country? What kind of a marriage did we want? What about fidelity now the illusion that the game kept all things public no longer existed? How to raise Elyse? How to bring Julie into our lives? How to reunite with families? What about friends? Should we continue to see Synanon people? Which Synanon people? All Synanon people? What about making new friends?

And then of course came the questions about Synanon. I was the first to realize I'd really split. I quit my job as a sales rep because I hated it and did it badly. Then I began a long, hard look at the whole experience, first horrified I'd lived that way for nineteen years, and then passionately curious about why. I sought separation from other Synanon people in order to discover my own true feelings about my life in Synanon—so I could make decisions about a variety of things.

How much did we want to know about the dark side? And then once we knew it, what did we do with the knowledge of what actually went on, our denial or complicity? And the divisions among Synanon people. It is my contention we went after each other instead of going after those truly accountable for the mess that was made. I'm not sure why this is so, but it is clear that it is what happened. There are many factions divided mainly over the way Synanon is retrospectively viewed. There is also a fair amount of reconstructionism. I don't know why I am so surprised. My sister had the exact same mother and father and then stepfather as I. We grew up in the same one bedroom apartment in Brooklyn for more than twenty years. We shared the same room, until I moved out when I was twenty-one, and yet you'd think we were raised in completely different households by our individual accountings.

ABOUT EVIL

I suppose I have unearthed more questions about both myself and Synanon in the process of writing this book than answers, but they are good questions. Was Chuck evil? To be sure, he was charismatic, charming, humorous, engaging, angry, addicted to alcohol, food and unobstructed power, manic depressive and hostile. I think all who knew him would agree, but what about evil? This is a difficult question, and after all I have read, Evelyn Kellman, a psychologist and writer I came to know after Synanon, talks about evil in a way that works for me. Following are her ideas I want to pass on to my children so they might be able to recognize the warning signs of what might be evil long before I did—so they might take flight.

I worry about them because evil wears clever disguises, and we have been trained to look for horns and tails and pitchforks. Evil doers are often more appealing than what we have been taught to look for.

It is almost impossible to label a person, other than Hitler, evil. Try it sometimes. Try putting that label on someone you know to have done bad things and see what happens. This word causes deep discomfort. We will throw out any label as an alternative. We will give the mean person the benefit of the doubt, do you think he really *intended* to...? We will take the more comfortable route of looking for the good in our enemies, and much prefer to attribute their behavior to madness. I long ago decided to eliminate the discussion of whether or not Chuck was evil except in my most private and personal pursuits of understanding.

Evil, because it is hard to see in another, must be measured by the feelings engendered by certain kinds of relationships. These relationships are often of unequal power and can be relationships with a parent, teacher, mate, therapist, religious leader—just about anybody. Evil can be present if you feel certain things or find yourself involved in certain ways of relating.

If someone makes you feel consistently confused or off balance in your dealings with him or her—i.e., they say they will do X but then do Y with no explanation or they declare a belief and then behave totally in opposition to that belief—beware. The key word here is consistent, not isolated, happenings that can be chalked up to misunderstandings. If your reaction to this person is to feel crazy and to begin to distrust yourself and what you have learned about the world and people, you might be in trouble.

If someone implies you need saving and talks to you from a place of righteousness indicating they know what is best for you, it would be wise to ask yourself what purpose your salvation or coming to his viewpoint serves him? Be on guard when someone who hardly knows you knows what is best for you. Why would you want to believe an other knows better than you what is best?

Evil wears disguises. It is a subtle force and evil doers adopt guises to hide their maliciousness. They often present themselves as giving and generous and back up these qualities with enough good acts to fool you. They often pose as being loving and wanting nothing but your good, but this can be their means of clouding your thinking and taking control. They are experts in blaming and sacrificing others for the imperfections they detect in themselves.

Perhaps the most destructive element in the relationship with evil is the process of developing self-doubt, suspending self-confidence, distrusting instincts and beliefs which leads to the destruction of your own early warning system. The most difficult decisions to be made in life are those that involve a conflict between your core morality and ethics and material reality. If you lose your sense of self you will be lost. I know.

There is no negotiating with evil. There is no reason. Your relationship with this person is not going to get better or resolve itself. There is only one action possible and that is flight. It is almost impossible to maintain firm boundaries around evil, and again evil is not only found in charismatic leaders, but in the workplace and all too often with heads of families.

I do not believe it is harsh to believe that evil exists. I believe it is foolish to pretend it does not exist, that all forms of behavior are explainable and healable. Ultimately evil is a force that works subtly in the disruption of another life force and against both the spiritual and intellectual growth of that other. It attempts to kill the spirit of a life, and sometimes the life itself.

It is almost impossible in a culture that so idealizes human value, while at the same time allowing needless human suffering, to label anyone evil without equal attention to forgiveness, healing and kindness. And that is why I find Evelyn Kellmen's thoughts so provocative. She focuses on you. She focuses on feelings that serve as warning signals evil might have penetrated your boundaries. Do not stick around to find out whether or not you are correct in your evaluation. We do not live in a court of law. You do not need proof your suspicions are correct. Do not wait. It is not worth it.

Whether or not Chuck was evil is not terribly important. The conversation about evil is what is important, because it helps each of us establish the boundaries necessary for our own spiritual comfort. It recognizes it is likely each of us will encounter evil in some form during our lifetime, and the conversation is one of the things that sharpens the tools we need to keep it away from us.

EX-ADDICTS

Jerry and I joke no matter what we do, we cannot get away from character disorders. Even when our lives look to be as squeaky clean and healthy as possible some surprise disorder invades our circle. Even one of our dogs, Sophie is, I am afraid, a character disorder. She simply has no conscience at all. Sometimes lovable, charismatic, aggressive and remorselessly badly behaved.

We spent twenty years in what we called, with pride, a totally integrated community. That often meant living with disordered people where the lowest common denominator ruled. As often as we asked disordered people to rise to higher expectations, we asked functioning people to lower standards. During one period, Jerry and I, who had never abused any substance, had to ask the local director, an ex-drug addict, permission if we wanted a glass of wine. This same director is presently a recovering addict—again. Jerry and I grew tired of it. After Synanon, we felt we'd spent entirely too much time in the company of people struggling with demons we barely understood and too often losing the battle. It is one thing to be surrounded with people like that if you can then go home at night, but we all lived in the same house. It got to be too close. When we left, we wanted to embark on other struggles. We wanted to get healthy, so we could put our energies into more life enhancing struggles.

I am at higher risk for cancer than others. I am at risk not only for the possibility of a recurrence, but at even higher risk to get cancer in my other breast. I cannot ignore that risk, and take the precautions I feel are sensible. I might get cancer anyway, but it would be foolish to throw caution to the winds and invite trouble.

Ex-dopefiends are also at high risk. Once an addict always the possibility of another addiction, and there is nothing sadder than someone who once triumphed over his addiction succumbing years later. It's not only the drugs or alcohol that become a problem. It isn't often someone maintains a good job, a good marriage, family and community responsibilities while he or she uses a little heroin on the side. Going down the tubes means just that—more than one tube, and it isn't pretty. Jerry and I find it difficult to include as our closest friends those who do not honor the addict part of their past.

GUILT AND SHAME

When I first decided to write about Synanon, I thought I would gather stories from a large group of people. I asked them to tell me something about life in Synanon that they found personally compelling. I thought if I was told stories of things that truly touched people about their experience in Synanon, I would come up with a well-rounded story. But there was something about almost all that was told that did not ring true, that seemed to skim the surface, and when I asked them to tell me what they thought was particularly compelling about the story, or why they chose that particular story, I was always surprised by their answers. I mostly thought otherwise, and realized I could not violate their trust by writing their stories with my endings.

For years I wondered about this and came up with a lot of answers that seemed true, but did not quite hit the mark. Why should they trust me with their most compelling stories? Why should they make themselves vulnerable to my scrutiny and interpretation? Why did I think everyone had to be on the same journey to finding the heart of Synanon I was? Wasn't everyone entitled to their own interpretation of their experience? Why didn't I just write about my own compelling experiences? Which is what I finally did.

But in so doing, I think I have figured out a more substantial answer to the original question of why most people told me less rather than more compelling stories. I think it has to do with the difference between guilt and shame.

It is easy for me to talk about my guilt. Guilt is about not having

229

taken responsibility. Guilt is about realizing the path not taken might have been the more responsible one. Guilt is about admitting my children needed more of me than I gave and wishing I had given more than I did, wishing I'd had more to give at that time. Guilt is about having turned my head to the left many too many times, when turning it to the right would have been the more responsible thing to do. The other side of guilt is about taking responsibility, and there is always an opportunity to take responsibility. You cannot undo the past, but you can take responsibility for it by holding yourself accountable, by apologizing and by creating space and time to make better decisions and take better paths in the present. So most people told me stories that had some element of guilt, or inspiration, and most often both.

Shame is another matter. Shame has to do with the pain of embarrassment, unworthiness and disgrace. It has to do with dishonor and great disappointment. We generally keep the events of our lives that brought us feelings of shame secret, often even from ourselves. Shame is more intimate than guilt and has to do with falling below our minimum standard of behavior or status. The system of meting out punishment, or more kindly, of administering object lessons in Synanon was based upon humiliation and shame. The superstructure of the community was continually dipping its hand into those arenas, while we, doing our daily tasks, found ourselves taking shameful situations and trying to play mind games with ourselves to turn them into "learning experiences."

Shortly after I put Elyse in the school, I was given the job of working with a group of young teenagers. I worked ten days straight and was off for ten days. My work day spanned fifteen hours, from 7:00 AM to 10:00 PM and contained a four-hour afternoon break. I was responsible for health, housing and some of the education of these children. The school was at Walker Creek in Tomales Bay, and on that property was a large laundry. The laundry contained commercial washers and dryers, and during the day a staff of people laundered the infants clothing, the infirmary linens and the laundry of the executive committee and board members who lived in Tomales Bay. When the professional laundry was closed, the machines were open to the community, which included the teenagers, who did their laundry unsupervised. It was thought they were old enough, had had enough supervision when they were younger, and those of us who disagreed were admonished to stop treating them like babies.

The rest of the community, including newcomers, also did their laundry in that same place, and as you can imagine, having had no real sense of ownership instilled in them, and being teenagers, clothing was not carefully attended to. This was also true of the newcomers. The difference was the children's clothing was recognizable because we inked their initials on collars, tags, waistbands or pockets when we distributed or bought clothing for them. At night, when the night man did his rounds, he gathered up all the leftover clothing in the laundry room, and because the only recognizable items belonged to the children, he bagged them and deposited them in one of their bunkhouses.

On the day I was assigned to this job, I inherited twelve huge, black garbage bags filled with clothing the night man had deposited in one of the children's bunkhouses for which I was responsible. Once again I was in the middle of clothing chaos. I had no idea of what to do, because once these clothes were properly distributed, whatever that meant, it was only going to happen again, and I did not want to take on the job of fixing the laundry room problem, which was a community, and not a school, issue.

I suggested to my boss the children be assigned a laundry time, and it be supervised, but she rejected that as coddling. On my second day of the job, the executive committee member responsible for property went on a tour with the two people who ran the school. He saw the twelve bags of clothing in the bunkhouse and gave them a "haircut" (dressing down). They immediately summoned me and gave me a rousing haircut. I was utterly humiliated and felt the stab of shame. I felt totally inadequate and substandard, especially since I could not figure out what to do about that mountain of clothing. It didn't matter that I had inherited a problem and the problem was simply a symptom of a systemic disease, which I knew to be the case. I responded only to the humiliation with feelings of intense shame. My intellect was easily subordinated to that intense emotion of shame.

I maintain these small episodes we all found ourselves in the middle of, from time to time, caused that same emotion in all of us, but we all thought no one could be as inadequate as we. The sad thing about being humiliated, possibly because of our early experiences with shame which usually surrounded toilet training and early socialization, is regardless of the circumstances if someone in authority tells you that you are substandard, you believe it and feel that same shame that was programmed at such an early age. This being the case, the use of humiliation is a valuable tool in an arsenal designed for control and manipulation.

Because shame is such a profoundly humiliating emotion, it is not surprising most were unwilling to share those core experiences with me. A couple did and one of them was Kathy.

DIRECT CONTACT WITH CHUCK

Kathy is a friend who shares her process with me—pretty or not. Both of us are carefully composed, yet are able to share humiliating details of our lives with comparative ease. It is Kathy's courage in looking into the shadows of her life that has inspired me to venture into my own. She wrestles with the truth, and once she finds it walks steadfastly in its path. She has dealt with many issues regarding shame and in sharing them with me has forged a kind of intimacy I find relatively few willing to engage in. Sharing shame brings that same vulnerability to the surface and it can be intimidating. But it is that vulnerability, that openness that creates trust and deep attachment.

Kathy is an artist who was on call for me when I was recovering from cancer surgery and treatment at the same time I was renovating my house. She is nothing short of a design genius, and when I had to make house decisions I was going to have to live with I called her. "Can you go with me to look at some tile? Could you take a look at some fabric?" She'd hop in a car and come. Every time.

Kathy gave me another wonderful gift last year when she sent me six pages of her experience working in the Lair (the name for Chuck's domain) directly for Chuck and Sharon. She told me these stories years ago, but they were fuzzy versions that contained only a hint of a truth she was not then comfortable with. She gave me the newer stories—stories of uncompromising focus—and told me I could use them however I wished in order to make my book work.

Kathy married into the Lair, which had been built and designed for Chuck and his wife, Sharon. This complex was attached to the Lodge at the Home Place and had access to both the lodge and the pool area. People were invited to the Lair, which was a big living room often used for parties, with adjacent offices, but most of us never went back into their living quarters. If you worked in the inner sanctum and were married to the person who managed Chuck's staff, which Kathy was, you got both an eyeful and earful of behind the scenes with the Dederichs. But no one is talking.

Kathy married Bill, who ran Chuck's personal staff. Bill was not an executive. He knew all of Chuck's quirks intimately, and he knew how to keep things as Chuck wanted them, from polished light bulbs to his reading glasses always being in exactly the same spot. He had no trouble repeating instructions over and over, and his ability to pay attention to minute detail was mythical.

Kathy suffered humiliation after humiliation while she was on Chuck's staff. Earlier, before Betty's death and changing partners, Kathy ran the school and Chuck's second wife, Sharon, worked for her. Kathy was both Sharon's boss and mentor in those earlier years and was clearly more intelligent, talented and intuitive when it came to working with children in spite of the fact Sharon had an advanced degree from a prestigious university. Kathy had no academic credentials, and shortly after changing partners, in the turbulence of Chuck's setting Sharon up to vie with Cicily as the most powerful woman in Synanon, Kathy entered the Lair as the newest kid on the block. Kathy is self-confident in her areas of competence, and she expresses herself with clarity and force in these areas. She saw herself as an ally to Sharon. Chuck, and possibly Sharon, saw her as a threat and the war began.

Kathy and Bill were summoned one morning at 3:00 AM to go with Chuck to Washington, DC when he feared authorities were after him during one or another of the investigations into criminal activities in Synanon. Chuck and a small group landed in Washington, DC with the intention of setting up headquarters and making Synanon available to the President of the United States for advice on the war on drugs and distribution of surplus goods. The truth about our stay in Washington is we were under surveillance the entire time we were there and finally left in disgrace, ultimately losing a major lawsuit involving an apartment building we purchased.

But when this small group arrived, with their packets of bran that they served themselves in restaurants, Chuck suffered severe culture shock after having been secluded and pampered and totally in charge of his and everybody's life for so long. He was outraged by the prices of things such as restaurant meals and hotels. He insisted at dinner, each couple share the salad upon which they spooned their bran, because of the outrageous prices. He demanded they leave their first hotel because the standards were so low he was certain he was going to have a heart attack. Bill's assignment was to find a better hotel that was also cheaper.

One evening after dinner, Bill and Kathy were sent out to find chocolate for Chuck. Stores were closed and, since they hardly knew this area, it took about an hour for them to return, chocolates in hand. They knocked on Chuck's hotel room door. He took the chocolates, screaming at them from behind the door they were useless and incompetent for taking so long. He was sending them back to California. They couldn't do anything right.

The next morning, at the front desk of the hotel, he bellowed at Bill he was useless and being married to Kathy was going to do him no good because she couldn't do anything. She was useless to him and therefore to Chuck. Outside the hotel he turned to her and yelled, "Useless, just useless." They were sent home and Bill's silence on the plane was deafening. He was pathologically connected to Chuck who meant everything to him, and there was nothing he would not do for the man. He could accept Chuck's rejections as small payment for the privilege of being so close, but being sent home had inflicted deep pain on him.

Chuck had designated himself and his executives and family "upstairs" as opposed to the rest of us who were "downstairs," and decided early on Kathy was simply not good enough for "upstairs." He told her this. He told this to Bill and he told it to Sharon. Business calls were made over the "wire" so everybody could hear. It was important to make things public "to get the word out." He interrupted the business calls Kathy made on the wire, correcting her to make her look like a fool. He was constantly accusing her in games, which were broadcast, of not having proper respect for Sharon, and he decided she was a sexual prude because she was uncomfortable about nude jacuzzis and having to be weighed in public in her underwear. He called her Sister Katherine, playing on the many years of Catholic school Kathy had attended.

Kathy had been certain the security she so wanted would now be hers, because she had come to be so close to the source. She was finally walking beside the man whose vision and words she had not only ardently believed, but had aggressively pursued in jobs she'd received generous recognition for. Kathy thought it would be safe here, and instead she was threatened with public humiliation at every turn.

Chuck and Sharon led relatively quiet lives until he went on some kind of rampage—angry about something—and then began a shake up, the public wire calls, the threats, the games, the housing moves, job changes, and then after about two weeks of upheaval back to his relatively quiet life as if nothing had happened—with lots of joking about people and events that had taken place in his manic state.

Kathy bought a pair of glasses. Chuck decided they looked too much like Sharon's glasses. Who did Kathy think she was? After all Sharon was educated and Kathy was not. How could it have been Sharon had once worked for Kathy? What kind of crazy decision had that been? Kathy was given the job of cleaning Chuck and Sharon's apartment, making their beds.

Chuck yelled at the staff for the smallest infractions. He could be just horrible, making them all feel as if they were insects, and then in a flash he would walk up to someone's desk, pick up the coffee cup, and say, "This coffee cup is not good enough for my staff. My staff is like my family, they deserve the best." He'd pile everyone into a van and have them taken into town to buy the best coffee cups available in the best store in Visalia.

Sharon gave Kathy art and furniture from the Lair to use in the housing she shared with Bill. It was called "storage in use," was considered a loan, but a loan of the best there was in Synanon. The rest of us used to be jealous those closest to Chuck had the best things, and there was a big gap between the quality of what they had and what the rest of us had. What we didn't know was Sharon would send other members of her staff for her stuff, without letting Kathy know, so Kathy would go home at the end of her work to find a big space on a wall where a painting had hung, or a chair or sofa missing. This happened regularly. Kathy would smile and act delighted at each offer, and then pretend it was okay when things in her possession were simply taken away. I remember seeing her wander through the meager stores of furniture searching for replacements.

Kathy never entertained that Chuck and Sharon were crazy. She just kept trying harder and harder to please, to prove to them she meant well, wanted to be helpful, wanted to learn. It couldn't be Chuck. She had to be the one who wasn't getting it. She had to try harder.

Sharon offered her fine china and linens and a special table so she and Bill could have a dinner party. Kathy set a beautiful table, and realized Sharon hadn't designated which cups she should use, so she chose some that matched the china and linens. Chuck and Sharon were walking through the lodge late in the afternoon before the dinner party and stopped to admire the table Kathy had set. Sharon mentioned she hadn't specifically told Kathy she could use those particular cups. Chuck had Kathy summoned from her rooms so they could position her, so they could yell at her for once again overstepping her bounds and forgetting her place.

Kathy's brother was killed in a tragic plane crash and she decided to go to the funeral which was unusual and nobody understood. To make matters even worse, her best friend who was married to one of Chuck's right hand executives, offered to go with her. This meant two people would be gone for two days, tying up a vehicle, staying at a hotel, spending money on food. It was a big deal. We simply did not do this kind of thing. Kathy was devastated by her brother's death; he was young and had a young family and it was a terrible tragedy. She needed and wanted support. To her credit, her friend stood up to unrelenting opposition and went anyway.

We now know Chuck was a manic depressive. We know he was an alcoholic, both a dry drunk, as they say in AA, and a using alcoholic. We have been told he suffered a series of small strokes that contributed to his possibly diminished capacity, but I never knew whether that was true or a ploy used to protect him from litigation. His behavior did become more and more erratic in the mid-eighties, but there were just a handful of people around him at that time, and the residents of the Home Place, who numbered about fifty, tried to stay out of his way. I was never close enough to see this side of him, and I always explained his rantings as his way of teaching object lessons; the result of his higher powers of consciousness. Who was I to question his methods? He was changing the world. He was saving lives. It was more than I was doing.

Kathy, like I, came looking for family and community in Synanon. She, like I, saw the promise of security as a dream come true. But Kathy saw something else when she first encountered Synanon when she was nineteen. She saw in the chaos of the creation of this new community an opportunity to develop the school. She was one of the earliest founders of the school and significantly impacted its formation. For all the school didn't do, it did provide a place for addict women to bring their children so they could at least be in the same place, and the children were better off than had they been with their addict parent or in foster care. Bringing children to Synanon was the only way of keeping newcomer women from leaving as they inevitably did if they had children on the outside. She also worked tirelessly at creating a place for the children of "squares" who were all too willing to turn over the care of their offspring to others. Kathy was a formidable presence in the school and received a lot of recognition for her work and, like the rest of us who worked in the school, made mistakes with children she would gladly take back if she could. Kathy had no children of her own. She was taking care of children whose parents placed them in her charge, parents in whom the larger responsibility for the way they were raised must reside.

The same thing that made Kathy such a force in the school makes her such a force as a friend and is the same thing that makes her pursue and hold on to the truth with such aggressive tenacity. I have been writing about Synanon for well over five years. I have interviewed a dozen people, and Kathy is the only one who told me of encounters with Chuck that resonated with the truth of his meanness close up. I suppose it is because what comes with that truth is humiliation and shame, and that is difficult to acknowledge—much less share.

CYCLES

My life moves in circles. I keep coming back to the same issues, and each time I seem to do a little better than the time before. But whenever something happens, such as an encounter with authority that leaves me somewhat unsettled, I am surprised. I'd thought I had that issue under control. Control is an illusion. It is only movement that is possible.

My mother is back in my life and my childhood gifts—salt and pepper shakers, water glasses and aprons—are being recycled into gifts of a different nature, gifts to help her better cope with aging alone. Today I find microwaves that fit on her counter and replace aging TV sets. I encourage her to get her groceries delivered and I communicate with doctors to help her cope with the full-blown disorders that were undiagnosed as well as unrecognized in her younger years. Agoraphobia, anxiety and depression work through her system and still she maintains complete independence tending with full intellectual competence to the affairs of her life. Our relationship has mellowed, but still, I have to be careful of the time we spend together. Too much time with her in that small apartment and the layers of my life melt leaving me feeling alone with the hopelessness of my childhood.

My marriage is as near perfect as a marriage can be. Jerry is an exceptional man full of patience and intelligence, and I attribute my side of the success to the twenty-odd years I spent figuring out how to get it right—round and round. I hurt people in the process, but it was the only way I knew to do it, and I'm probably no worse than most for the harm caused. Life is not simple and relationships are anything but simple. Happiness isn't always calm and constant. Contentment comes in spurts. Change is always turbulent, and change and risk are an intrinsic part of growth. Every once in a while I look up from a place of deep contentment and realize it is time for an adventure. I have become good at this, and instead of throwing all cards in the air, I choose one or two and move in the direction they land. It seems so simple. I wonder why I thought it was okay to throw all the cards at once, would have done nothing less. When I moved into Synanon, I took the wedding album from my first marriage and threw it in a dumpster. Why would I do that? No more pictures of Alice as Jackie Kennedy. My grandparents all dressed up. My mother younger than I am today. My first husband's little old aunts that he made such fun of. All that observable history lost.

Jerry and I joke that between the two of us we make one good parent. I wonder at my good fortune that both of my daughters seem to want me deeply into their lives and are willing to put their hurt and anger at not having had more constant mothering into a small corner of their large hearts. I have tried hard to establish a new intimacy because we will never have the intimacy that day-to-day growing up together creates. I see it in my friends' families.

241

Susan's twenty-six-year-old daughter facing personal crises and loss came home to cry for an entire week. Susan and her husband took turns comforting their daughter until she was able to come up with a plan and move on. I wonder if my girls will ever have that kind of trust in me; will ever seek that kind of comfort from my home. Who knows? We have as many chances to right wrongs as we do to commit them. They have so much life ahead of them, and I have a lot more to give now than I did when they were little.

I doubt that there is anyone my age that can look back and come up ninety-five percent on the positive side of the ledger. And if they can, I fear they might be a bit uninteresting. It makes no sense to dwell on the negative, but it makes equally little sense to ignore it. I moved into Synanon with many things wrong. Had I been more whole I would not have chosen such a restrictive life. Had I been healthier I would not have chosen to be yelled at ritually several times a week. The job of Synanon was to keep people in their places so the work of Synanon could be done. I wish I had believed my place could have been so much bigger than the slot I chose. I will forever be amazed at my amazement that my life was so improved the minute I left Synanon. With little money, no material possessions, a thirteen-year-old child who had never lived closely with adults, a nineteen-year-old who was angry at my sudden intrusion into her life—many stresses and fears— Jerry and I set out to build a life, and in so doing developed great intimacy and friendship and have been able to reach goals I couldn't even daydream about when I lived in Synanon. How can that be?

Synanon only looks restrictive to me from the fortunate position I now occupy. It never seemed restrictive during the years I was trying to figure out how to be responsible in the world; during the years I practically flung myself from one relationship to another; during the years I moved in and out of parenting two healthy children who deserved much more from me than they got. I desperately needed family and community, and since I had neither in the sense that I needed them, Synanon promised not only what I so needed, but its promises were the stuff of dreams. And after nineteen years, I emerged with my tiny family and not much community to speak of. I was in almost the exact same place regarding family and community that I was when I moved in to Synanon, the difference being that I had resources I didn't have back then. I have had to be the one to create my own community. It was a jolt to realize that no one was going to draw me into theirs. It was slow. First there was the establishment of Thanksgiving as the holiday I would make happen. Then there was the planning for every milestone; birthdays, anniversaries, job promotions. Two weddings and the introduction of sons into our immediate family. Now grandchildren are on the horizon. My circle is not as large as I had anticipated, but it is sturdy. A few good friends, and a decent extended family surround us. It's not what I imagined, but it is better than I ever dreamed I could have.

The best thing about being ten years removed from Synanon is that the kind of denial and wishful thinking, the brainwashing and fear motivation, the thinking that brought me too close to activities and behaviors I should have fled from no longer seems so peculiar and extreme. A cult is a wonderful window through which these kinds of thinking and behaviors glare out. We were isolated and we were pretty extreme. But after ten years of life outside that restricted community, I find that kind of distorted thinking, to greater or lesser degrees, more common than uncommon. I find people blindly following the dictates of bosses, mates, and the culture in general, but in situations so commonplace that few feel compelled to examine them.

One man who earns a great deal of money for a sexy and glitzy organization is jerked all over the country to meetings at a moment's notice with no regard for the fact that he has twin toddlers and a working wife. He once flew the red-eye across the country for a morning meeting and after waiting around all day to be called in was finally told they wouldn't have time for him and would he please return in two days. This was not an isolated occurrence. Another friend who also earns a staggering salary is subject to Monday morning meetings at which the boss picks one of the executives each week to berate, humiliate and scream at. Each Monday he anxiously prepares for the meeting never knowing which meeting will be on him. The same boss moves between friendly interest in his executives and temper tantrums during the course of the workday. His executives walk around with knots in their chests. They do it because he pays them extravagant salaries. I can't tell you the number of women I've talked to who stayed in marriages in which deceit, lies and gross inequalities of power were part of their contractual arrangement. When the marriages ended, mostly because the man wanted out and only sometimes because the woman realized what was going on, the women said similar things to what I said after I left Synanon. What was I thinking?

Then there is the big brainwashing about male–female things. Masculinity and femininity. The entire issue surrounding the size and age of the "ideal" woman should prove my point. The "ideal" woman is approximately twenty-three years old and weighs somewhere around one hundred pounds regardless of her height. She has big breasts, which she has surgically installed if hers are not the correct size. I'd like to find a handful of women who are honestly free of this very successful brand of cultural brainwashing. All of this is not to say that I let myself off the hook for having been dense and uncritical about my life. It is simply to say I am not as alone in this as I once thought.

Life for me has sorted out well which is not to say that I don't have problems and lots of growth and challenge ahead of me. I feel confident that I can do a better job of handling the future because I have surrounded myself with helpful people. I consider that no small accomplishment.

The trouble with writing such a book about a specific period in my life, even a period with all the drama of Synanon, is next year I will feel differently about much of what I write today. I have been writing about my life in Synanon for over five years and what I think and feel has shifted more than the California earth beneath me. But it is time for me to put this all to rest. There is other work to be done.

EPILOGUE

Ten plus years have passed since the writing of this book. In that time I have completed graduate school, achieving a Masters in Spirituality and Holistic Health with a specialty in Transpersonal Psychology. My husband and I have built a business which we are presently handing over to a new generation. I stand by most of what I wrote in the first edition of this book and am pretty impressed that I was able to do it as well as I did, so close to the experience. With time, the experience of Synanon has become but one of many experiences. It has grown smaller and yet continues to impact my life almost daily.

There are three things I would like to add to my story because they have crystallized over the years and so the story is somewhat changed.

First, I want to say something about the way I feel about Cicely, Chuck's daughter. My transference with her was about ME. She triggered emotions I had stored since childhood as a result of my mother's behavior toward me. Triggers really have little to do with the person who triggers. What I learned from that transference was valuable. I have been truly humbled by the actions Cicely has taken to make amends for whatever bad feelings people have for her as a result of her role in Synanon. She has been incredibly honest and self-reflective, and I have seen her extend herself and embrace the values she now holds dear. She was a major victim of Synanon's wrongs and she has taken full responsibility for trying to right whatever wrongs she might have committed. I have nothing but admiration for her.

When I wrote the first edition, I did not fully realize how troubled I had become in the years before I moved into Synanon. I was in a failing marriage that I had entered in spite of many red flags. I had had a child in this very shaky situation. I was completely without support, except for these new people from Synanon who opened their arms to me. I had no money and although I had a teaching credential I did not have the resources to support myself and my child either within my marriage or outside of it. Looking back, I can fully understand how someone might ask why I didn't just get a job, find a place to live and some scrappy furniture, and cobble together child care—as scores of others in my situation had done. It is difficult for me to say this, but I couldn't do that. This flies in the face of my image of myself as a competent, can-do, figure-it-out person. But I was not competent and could not figure it out. Synanon saved me, just like it saved many others who could not manage their lives in a meaningful way. It saved me by being there and saying yes to me.

I wish I could put this all together for you, the reader, as well as for myself, but all I can say is that judging others by your own standards doesn't work. How many times have I wondered why so-and-so didn't just do something that seemed so easy to me. *If she needs work, why doesn't she just take ANY job? Why doesn't she just leave him—she has the resources?* But I cannot judge them, because I cannot answer why, when my life wasn't working, I saw moving into this wildly different community as my only alternative. And I also cannot answer why, after I lost custody of my magnificent child, I didn't leave the community to take care of her. I am no longer interested in offering my insights into why others make the decisions they make. I can never understand why someone can't do something that seems so obvious to me, just as I cannot explain why I was unable to do things that seem completely reasonable to others. The best I can come up with is that my decisions were made from a place of survival. I was so far out of my comfort zone that my primitive brain took over and I could see no other solution. I no longer expect a neat understanding of my earlier choices and I no longer harshly judge others who seem to be stumbling around unable to solve their dilemmas. How can I ever understand someone else's process if I can hardly understand my own?

The second takeaway from my Synanon experience is relevant to today's political climate and the rise of Donald Trump. I am astonished that a person who is blatantly racist, xenophobic, dishonest, self-serving, dictatorial and mean-spirited is president of our magnificent country. I have been both grieving the loss of decorum and fearing the outcome of the damage he is doing. I despair when I see how our country has become addicted to the *drama of Trump*. I find I am being drawn into it myself, in spite of hating it so. But what makes it worse is that I understand the people who are supporting him so well.

If I have learned nothing else from the experience of Synanon and my subsequent studies, I have learned that *what we want to believe trumps all reality*. I so wanted to believe in Synanon, in its vision, in the goodness and generosity of its founder that I was able to deny my core values over and over. Something would hit me in the solar plexus as not quite right and I would immediately rationalize by focusing on *my* wrongness, *my* lack of understanding—and amazingly that gut feeling would diminish as I adopted whatever "truth" was being

249

presented to support what I had intuited as wrong. There is no way for me to explain this to someone who hasn't experienced it.

I cannot imagine that today anyone could convince me to leave my husband, have my tubes tied, eat what I don't want to eat, do exercises I don't want to do, allow myself to be yelled at and diminished—which are the very things that we agreed to in Synanon. But I did. And because of this I can understand that even though people may think they could never have lived in such a system, in fact they *could* have and some of them are.

Many people right now are twisting their minds to accept policies that are going to hurt them in the long run. It has become easier and easier to embrace the "truth" we like as opposed to the "truth" that is the best information we have at the present moment. When I was in Synanon and a relative would visit and comment on things they saw, I disregarded them as being "unenlightened" and too dense to understand—and besides, they would soon leave and I wouldn't have to continue to hear their side. Relations with outsiders were discouraged and we were so busy moving and changing that we mostly had no one to listen to but one another, and this constantly reinforced the group's values over my own.

We live in a post-modern world where hard facts and truth have become less hard, where space and time are artificial and fluid, where boundaries are less clear. I like all of this because I think it opens us to more information and expanded consciousness. But this does not mean truth is just a big free-for-all, an M&M bag full of "truths"… pick the flavor that you like best. There is still truth and falsehood; there is still better and less good information. There are people who actually know things and their knowledge is important to be open to.

Everybody eventually left Synanon—the organization no longer exists. But not everyone actually left the Synanon mindset. Almost thirty years after the end of Synanon there are still people thinking the way we did in the Synanon community. It gives me pause regarding the state of our nation. I hope we make it.

And finally, my big takeaway. In one of the rooms at Pacific Pearl, which is where the doctors I like best work, there is a banner. It says there are only three things that are important.
1. Kindness
2. Kindness
3. Kindness
I grew up in a household that did not display much kindness. I was yelled at. From the time I was eleven until I married at twenty-one, there were many, many months when at least one of our four family members in the house was not speaking to another. It was harsh and there was little emotional nourishment. My mother was also predictably unpredictable. I knew a storm was coming, I just couldn't always predict when.

Synanon too was harsh. Its practice of "the Game" was harsh. People were spoken to harshly outside of the game as well. There were unpredictable punishments—housing moves, demotions, the wearing of signs as a means of humiliation. This was all designed to keep a pretty diverse and unlikely group under control.

But that is not the life I live now. No one yells. My husband is a loving, kind, generous man who has my back at all times. My children are lovely people who I cannot find enough wonderful things to say about. My grandkids are bright lights.

I have learned to love unconditionally and find it far more rewarding than setting conditions and making judgments. My final understanding is that a place of kindness and generosity is the only place to be. Life is all about love. Synanon, for all of its visionary ideals, was not that place. I have devoted this final part of my life to living in love and giving up fear. All of that other stuff—the lack of kindness, the judgment, etc.—comes from fear. Finding myself well on the road to living in love, I can say unequivocally that love definitely trumps fear.

ABOUT THE AUTHOR

Alice Rost was born and educated in New York. She grew up in a working class neighborhood in Brooklyn, graduated from New York University and taught elementary school. In 1966 she moved to California.

Alice became involved with Synanon about six months after she arrived in California and became a resident of Synanon in 1970. She was twenty-eight when she moved in, with her nine-month-old baby daughter, and left nineteen years later. After that she and her husband lived in San Diego where they owned a business.

Alice was a spiritual seeker, teacher and devoted disciple. She wrote her first book about her time at Synanon, *Designated Dancers*, published in 2001. After earning her degree in Spirituality and Holistic Health with a specialty in Transpersonal Psychology at age seventy-five, she wrote and published her second book, *Awakening to God: Not a Man in the Sky*, published in 2018.

Exquisite self-care and her spiritual practice carried her through two cancers, which she claimed were "quiet" while she lived a robust life. Two more books were created from her *Yearly Letters* to her grandchildren, although she did not live to deliver them personally. This revised edition of *Designated Dancers* is being published posthumously as well. Alice succumbed to a third and final bout with a rare blood disorder in 2019. She will be deeply missed.

CPSIA information can be obtained
at www.ICGtesting.com
Printed in the USA
BVHW081044180620
581804BV00001B/57

9 781929 909186